ADMISSIONS ESSAY BOOT CAMP

ADMISSIONS ESSAY BOOT CAMP

How to Write Your Way into the Elite College of Your Dreams

ASHLEY WELLINGTON

TEN SPEED PRESS

Berkeley

Copyright © 2014 by Ashley Wellington

Published in the United States by Ten Speed Press, an imprint of the Crown Publishing Group, a division of Random House LLC, a Penguin Random House Company, New York.
www.crownpublishing.com
www.tenspeed.com

Ten Speed Press and the Ten Speed Press colophon are registered trademarks of Random House LLC.

Library of Congress Cataloging-in-Publication Data

Wellington, Ashley.
  Admissions essay boot camp : how to write your way into the elite college of your dreams / Ashley Wellington.

    pages cm

    Summary: "This top-tier college admissions essay guide replicates a brainstorming and essay-writing session with Mint Tutors founder Ashley Wellington"— Provided by publisher.

1. College applications—United States—Handbooks, manuals, etc. 2. Universities and colleges--United States—Admission—Handbooks, manuals, etc. 3. Exposition (Rhetoric)—Handbooks, manuals, etc. 4. Essay—Authorship—Handbooks, manuals, etc. I. Title.

  LB2351.52.U6W45 2014

  378.1'616—dc23

                              2014005258

Trade Paperback ISBN: 978-1-60774-612-6
eBook ISBN: 978-1-60774-613-3

Printed in the United States of America

Front-cover photograph copyright © Mega Pixel/Shutterstock.com
Author photo copyright © Roger Kriegel
Design by Margaux Keres

10 9 8 7 6 5 4 3 2 1

First Edition

FOR PARKER

CONTENTS

WHAT DO YOU KNOW ABOUT IT?

+ HOW THIS BOOK IS DIFFERENT +

When I first started working with students on their college essays, I found that many of their parents would come to me with stacks of books on the subject. Those guides normally fell into one of two categories:

+ Essays that "worked" at certain Ivy League schools
+ Simple steps for getting the essay over with as quickly as possible

Although it is immensely helpful to read well-written personal statements and see the different approaches you can take in your own applications, I don't think the winning essay books tell the whole story, because they don't give you any context. Basically, without knowing the background, credentials, and interests of the student who wrote it, you can't see why the essay was successful in the first place. College essays don't exist in isolation; they enhance and explain the transcript.

As for the "steps" category, I love making lists as much as (and possibly more than) anyone, but trying to crank out a formulaic essay in an hour or two is not the right approach for a top-tier application. Unfortunately, if you're shooting high, you can't sound like everyone else, and you can't get away with an expedient effort.

In short, I've tried to combine everything I've found helpful in other books while still personalizing the process so you feel as if you're working one-on-one with me. This book will give you the full "Boot Camp" experience, from start to finish, without any sugar coating. You have to put time into your essays, but the payoff is great!

WHAT'S THE ESSAY GOT TO DO WITH IT?

If you have picked up this book, you are probably in your junior or senior year of high school, which means it is impossible to augment or change what is already on your transcript. But take a deep breath. This guide is meant to show you how to successfully work with what you have. Six hundred and fifty words about (virtually) anything really *can* get you into the college of your dreams, as long as you remember my three H's:

+ Humility
+ Honesty
+ Humor

I am going to personally walk you through the confusing, intimidating, and stressful process of drafting the perfect college application essay. Along the way, I will demonstrate the difference between a clever approach, a gimmick, and an application self-destruct button. Then I will give you some more insights I've gleaned over the years. Remember, there is no specific right answer, but there are many, many wrong answers.

Still need convincing? Here is the more erudite version:

The essay is the keystone to an application, and as such, it can function as either an asset or a liability. Most essays are predictable, innocuous, and forgettable and do nothing to set you apart from the rest of a talented applicant pool. Bad essays—in which you come across as someone who lacks motivation, perspective, or passion—can severely hurt your chances. On the other hand, an original response to an essay question offers an immeasurable boost to your admission chances. College essays do more than just showcase your writing ability; ideally, they illustrate your priorities, admirable traits, creativity, and academic promise.

Every year, the number of students applying to college increases, and each student applies to a greater number of schools. As a result, colleges and universities can have between ten and fifteen qualified applicants vying for a single spot, and in many cases the students have comparable test scores, grades, and extra-curricular interests. College essays are swiftly becoming the most significant part of an application because they often are the only variable in the admissions equation. All schools, particularly the smaller ones, have their own unique personalities, and admissions committees want to know whether you'd be a good fit for the campus environment and current student body. The essay is now the determining factor.

Mastering the college essay is somewhat of a lost art in our sound-bite culture. So often, students are intimidated by the very idea of college and end up writing only what they think admissions committees might want to hear. Whether that means assuming an overly scholarly tone, discussing a backpacking trip as a metaphor for life (ugh), or debating the intricacies of global warming in Al Gore's *An Inconvenient Truth* when nothing else on your application points to an interest in environmentalism, these attempts often fall flat. The best essays are unapologetically *you*. They aren't trying to be the next great American novel; they are simply an account of something personally significant, written in a concise and compelling way.

Although the concept of writing a college essay, in which you articulate fundamental qualities you possess, is often an intimidating challenge, it's also a fantastic opportunity to tell admissions officers why they should choose you. The prompts are intentionally broad, so you can play up your strengths *on your own terms*. Aside from word count, the guidelines dictate little about format, topic, voice, or tone, so you can employ your own style and discuss episodes from your life that address the essay topics with originality and confidence.

There are countless urban legends about successful college essays that made a difference for otherwise ordinary applicants. A favorite among guidance counselors goes like this: Once upon a time, a question on the Harvard application asked students to give a definition of courage based on their personal experiences. One student simply wrote, "This is courage" as his answer and mailed it in. You don't have to be this gutsy to stand out; all you have to do is be yourself.

For this book, I've provided and commented on many real essays that helped students gain admission to some of the country's top colleges and universities, listed step-by-step processes for getting ideas down on paper, and written detailed student profiles so you can see the writing process in action for the most commonly used essay topics. I've even classified responses by student type so you can identify with essay approaches based on your own experiences and background. The student profiles and essays have all been tweaked to protect the students' privacy—names of high schools, summer programs, and teachers have all been changed or omitted, and the students themselves have been given pseudonyms—but everything else remains authentic.

One more thing to bear in mind: Your essay is not just a laundry list of your accomplishments. Admissions officers have access to your grades and activities. If you've won awards, they will know about them, so there's no need for you to fire them off as if you walk on water in your spare time just for kicks. **The only things they don't know are the type of person you are, how you handle success, and how you relate to others.**

CHAPTER 1

WHERE IT ALL BEGINS

+ IDENTIFYING YOUR STUDENT TYPE +

This chapter will help you figure out what type of applicant you are, so that you know the best way to present yourself on paper. Don't be concerned if you fit into more than one of these categories. You'll see later on that the students outlined in the "Make It Unique" chapter sometimes fall under multiple headings, and all have distinct stories to tell. Classifying yourself just makes it easier to determine the most effective approach for you—and you better believe that colleges will be trying to put a label on the type of student you are. You might as well use this to your advantage. Also, most of you will fall into the Achieve-o-Tron, Natural, and Club President student types, because you have the drive and the academic pedigree to attend top-tier colleges and universities. Without further ado, here they are.

1. THE ACHIEVE-O-TRON

When your classmates complain that they have too much work to do or too many activities on their plates, their parents will turn to them and say, "Oh yeah? Then how come [*your name here*] is getting straight A's in six AP classes, is All-State in three different sports, is student body president, a nationally ranked debater, and the first-chair violinist of the school orchestra?" You are that notorious paragon, the pinnacle of high school achievement. Teachers admire you and have probably asked you to serve as a peer leader or even to organize an after-school tutoring program. Your parents have plastered the walls of your home with spelling bee plaques and framed National Latin Exam certificates. In fact, you have accumulated so many accolades that you will run out of space to list them on your Common Application, and when you meet with your school college guidance counselor, he or she will probably ask, "Which Ivy League school have you chosen to attend?" not "What are your reaches, targets, and safeties?"

You definitely deserve to take pride in your many talents, but that doesn't mean you are such a shoo-in to a top-tier school that your essay is negligible. In fact, it means the opposite. Think about it. There are approximately thirty-seven thousand high schools in the country, which puts you up against thirty-seven thousand other valedictorians, not counting home-schooled students, and an additional, let's say, seventy-four thousand high achievers who look almost exactly like you do on paper. Admissions officers are looking for reasons to toss your impossibly perfect application onto the heap of "no" files, so feeding them a smug, tedious, or predictable essay will make their jobs much too easy. *Your imperative*: show them something totally unexpected, perhaps an experience where you failed. Don't take yourself too seriously. *Your angle*: humility.

2. THE DABBLER

Have you ever heard someone refer to college as the magical time when you get to try a slew of new classes and clubs in an effort to figure out what to do with the rest of your life? Unfortunately, you get no such luxury in high school. At age eighteen or so, you are given the gift of four years to home in on the best channel for your strengths, but for some reason, at age fourteen, you are expected to specifically pinpoint your "true passion" in order to have material for a strong college admissions application at the end of high school. Then you must immediately make it the focal point of your academic schedule, pursue related extracurricular activities so that you can qualify for leadership positions in your junior and senior years, spend your summers engaging in competitive internships, and perhaps even carry out an independent research project on the subject, all to demonstrate what colleges deem the necessary "depth, not breadth" factor.

Obviously, not every teenager can carry out this unrealistic master plan. And so, in an effort to find yourself, you sampled a variety of activities. You joined the basketball team but made second-string junior varsity, and after toughing it out for a season you decided it wasn't the best use of your time. You auditioned for the school musical in your freshman year but didn't feel passionate enough about the experience to reprise your role as "townsperson #7" in your sophomore spring. You spent two years attending monthly meetings for your school's seventy-four-person Investor's Club but never really dove in. You enrolled in a semester of ceramics, then two semesters of figure drawing, and finally capped off your fine arts requirement with a brief stint in choir.

You are decent at everything, but you haven't found your niche, and now you're facing an uphill battle trying to convince colleges that the only thing standing between you and your total commitment to an academic or extracurricular trajectory is access to their unique programs. You also need to address your lack of depth without sounding defensive and instead present it as an endearing aspect of your personality. *Your imperative*: show your undaunted dedication to a single endeavor, so you don't appear aimless. *Your angle*: an inquisitive mind, a desire to explore, and an ability to commit when you find things that interest you.

3. THE ATHLETE

You can hold your own in the classroom, but you're not exactly the student in the front row whose eternally raised hand is blocking everyone else's view of your teacher's PowerPoint presentation on DNA replication. You get your work done and make decent grades, but academic achievement may not be your primary focus. The places where you do stand out, though, are on the court and the field, and especially in your school newspaper's sports section, where you are profiled or mentioned on almost a weekly basis. Known as a triple threat, you are captain of three different varsity sports, have been voted MVP in each since your junior year, have earned All-State honors more than once, and have twelve pins clustered on your varsity letter jacket. You were even homecoming king or queen. But your school is part of a relatively small conference, one that isn't exactly a hotbed of recruiting activity, and besides, you know that only around 2 percent of student athletes are awarded athletic scholarships.

Do you want to play a sport in college? Absolutely. But you don't want to go to a lower-rung school simply because it has offered you a spot on the team. In fact, as much as you love sports, you (or perhaps your parents) would rather your athletic accomplishments be used to help you gain admission to a higher-caliber college. You're okay with warming the bench for a season or two, because you're realistic about the importance of a good education in today's competitive job market. After all, if you had been recruited, the application process would be more of a formality for you, but unfortunately, that's not the case. *Your imperative*: show that you have brains in addition to brawn. *Your angle*: ideally, an intellectually stimulating undertaking such as an independent research project, a fascinating elective that changed your perspective, or a book with ideas that challenged you. If your transcript is limited, make sure you discuss sports through a scholarly lens. In general, it's time to show off your cerebral side!

4. THE CLUB PRESIDENT

At your school's club fair every September, do you find that you are spread too thin as you rotate among the different booths, talking up the perks of the Young Investors' Club, the Python Programming Club, and the Flamenco Dance Appreciation Society to throngs of wide-eyed freshmen? You recognized early on that physical education was not your strongest subject, so instead of joining a sports team, you channeled your extracurricular time and energy into various clubs. Before entering high school, you were told by parents and teachers alike that earning leadership positions was key to a successful college application, and you took this advice quite seriously. If there's one thing you have in abundance, it's titles, from president to cultural chair. Feeling limited by your school's list of established, recognized, and sponsored clubs, you've even created a few of your own organizations, all with the approval of certain administrators and the requisite signatures of your peers. You may think you've gamed the system and demonstrated both depth *and* breadth in your transcript, seeing as how you're committed to many diverse interests. Your academic record is reasonably strong to boot: you may not be valedictorian, but you're holding your own in a number of challenging AP classes. It's no surprise that, going into the college admissions process, you're feeling pretty confident.

As with your other heavily involved classmates, you should absolutely feel proud of your accomplishments and effort, but you've actually put yourself in a difficult position. Admissions committees are going to have no idea what to make of you or what you'd bring to the table. You're in better shape than, say, the Dabbler, but an excess of activities actually dilutes your credibility and makes you appear scatterbrained. It is impossible to decipher what really makes you tick, unless it's the titles themselves, and that's an empty angle for your essays. *Your imperative*: there's no getting around your extracurricular record, so instead of focusing on a single activity for your personal statement, have a clear focus and find a unifying theme that can highlight a positive personal trait. *Your angle*: an open and curious mind, as well as an outgoing nature.

5. THE AVERAGE JOE

Now, there are two types of Average Joes: those who have struggled to stand out and are starting to get their footing, albeit a little late in the game, and those who are apathetic underachievers. I am speaking only to the former category, since no college counselor has the energy for someone who either doesn't care or isn't willing to try. You differ from the Dabbler in that you've stuck with the same activities for several years, but while you're pretty good at everything, you haven't found a category in which you stand out. You're a B student, a junior varsity athlete, a staff member rather than an editor for your school newspaper, and an alternate for the math league. Your school is probably large, with several hundred students per grade, so the sheer numbers make it harder to be extraordinary and easier to be anonymous.

But you care, and that's what's important. In your junior year, you fell in love with physics even though the class threatened to sink your GPA at several points along the way, and you stayed in one Saturday night to read *The Pleasure of Finding Things Out* by Richard Feynman. You applied to a six-week science and math summer program but didn't get accepted, and you failed to come up with a less competitive backup plan, so you spent your summer working at a local sporting goods store instead. You're starting to show journalistic promise now that you've been assigned to cover the "Features" section, but it's too late to rise in the ranks.

You want to go to a top-tier college, or perhaps your parents are insistent that you go, but you're feeling discouraged and pessimistic, especially when you compare yourself to last year's overachieving seniors who were rejected or wait-listed. It's important to be realistic, but that doesn't mean you should give up. There are still ways to win over admissions committees with a poignant narrative. *Your imperative*: acknowledging that you are a late bloomer and expressing how excited you are to have found an activity or subject where you know you can shine. *Your angle*: anticipation. You will, ideally, show the measures you are taking to dive deeper into the pursuit and explain how you plan on expanding it.

6. THE NATURAL

While it's hard to imagine a scenario in which being gifted might hold you back, you are so smart and talented that you can get by with minimal investment in your classes or school community —and that's a bad thing. You realized from a young age that you didn't really have to study for tests, and you don't enjoy club meetings because you grow bored listening to what you consider petty bickering over the best way to allocate the organization's $50 in bake sale proceeds. You may feel somewhat isolated from your classmates, and although your teachers grow annoyed with your tendency to doodle and window-gaze in the back corner seat of the classroom, you silence them with your insights each time they try to catch you in a daydream. The good news is, being bored by your high school curriculum is a strike against you only if you haven't sought enrichment elsewhere. In some cases, being in the 99th percentile is enough to land you a coveted acceptance letter from your top choice school, but more often than not, you still have to show that you care about something—anything. *Your imperative*: you may come off as bored in the classroom, but you must show that you are both interesting and interested. You need to apply your talents to an endeavor that allows you to be something other than a brainiac, so figure out the best channel for all that mental power. *Your angles*: humility and dedication.

7. THE UN-NATURAL

A mix of the Achieve-o-Tron and Average Joe student types, the Un-Natural doesn't have the talent to catapult to the top, but still earns a spot in honors classes through tireless studying. If you're an Un-Natural, you are beyond organized, taking color-coordinated margin notes in your textbook with a bevy of bright pens and flipping through flash cards on your way to class while other students check their text messages. You are a master of dates, names, and times, which is why you get nervous before in-class essays or tests that are based on analysis and idea application, not fact recall. You may sometimes get frustrated with your more cerebral peers who discuss politics or abstract art while you hole-punch your highlighted handouts to neatly file into your binders, but you take all the same classes that they do, and you are holding on to your A– average, so you have nothing to be ashamed of. In fact, the Un-Natural should be extremely proud of his or her abilities to be goal-oriented and dogged. However, Un-Naturals often encounter one or more of the following problems: they are so fixated on their grades that they let their extracurricular commitments fall to the wayside, their parents have chosen their activities for them, or they don't have an experience or interest that they can discuss with any depth. Don't worry, though. While colleges want, ideally, a combination of talent and drive, having only the latter is not a deal breaker. *Your imperative*: show an activity or topic that really gets you intellectually excited. Colleges want to see that you are capable of digging beneath the surface and applying yourself to something because you love it, not just because you get rewarded with grades. *Your angle*: enthusiasm.

8. THE SECRET PRODIGY

Your classmates have no idea who you are, and your parents have probably reprimanded you for the lackluster feedback they've received during parent-teacher conferences. You're smart, though, which is why everyone is so frustrated with what they interpret as your apathy. You score well on standardized tests, but nothing at your school has ignited your interest.

It's off campus where you thrive and shine. You are an expert in astronomy and spend hours cataloging the stars through your telescope, then poring over the writings of Galileo and Hubble. You are learning ancient Greek in your spare time to gain more insights into the beliefs espoused by the Stoic philosophers. Or perhaps you are devoted to your community service troupe that performs skits at other local schools to educate students on resisting peer pressure and the dangers of recreational drug use. Regardless, these interests will not show up on your transcript, so you must find a way to highlight them in your essay. *Your imperative*: demonstrate how your devotion to independent endeavors contributes to your academic life, so admissions officers know you'd be a great asset to their college classrooms. With individual activities, you always have to make sure you add a community emphasis. *Your angles*: curiosity and commitment.

9. THE BUDDY

You are the definition of likeable: outgoing, laid-back, and above the drama that normally permeates high school hallways. You have a multitude of friends, and even those who don't know you very well feel comfortable sitting down with you in the cafeteria. Occasionally, though, you may be a little too easygoing and lack drive. Your parents might even have to push you to add academic activities to your packed social calendar, which can be a problem when it comes to college admissions.

The Buddy student type is always paired with another category, so your grades and athletic skills vary across the board, but all Buddies have an admirable and uncanny ability to connect with others, and that's something worth stressing in an essay. *Your imperative*: whether you're discussing a community service project, a camping trip, or a debate in your AP U.S. history class, make sure you show how well you relate to others and bring people together. *Your angle*s: extroversion and affability.

10. THE ARISTOCRAT

While the other types on this list have defined students by their behaviors and skills, this category relates solely to a student's background. Unfortunately, I have to include it here because many affluent high schoolers don't grasp the extent of their privilege, and understandably so: it is all they have known. As a result, they unintentionally write bratty essays that dash their college dreams. When your transcript testifies to the fact that you come from a certain zip code, attend an elite private school, and have parents who are neurosurgeons, lawyers, investment bankers, or CEOs, admissions officers will be able to glean a lot about your background. Having such resources is an incredible gift as long as you made the most of them and possess some perspective. In short, don't brag about vacations you've been able to take, name-drop your well-connected family friends, or talk about anything that came to you without effort. *Your imperative*: do not try to demonstrate hardship or feel sorry for yourself in any way. Instead, show your values, such as a strong work ethic and loyalty. *Your angle*: humility, humility, humility!

Did you feel a little tingle as you read these ten student types, because you realized that one or more of them described you to a T? Good! Now you have a solid starting point, and you know, at least thematically, how you should be presenting yourself. Catering to your student type will definitely help admissions officers to favorably interpret the rest of your application. Remember: let them get to know you on your terms.

CHAPTER 2

BRAINSTORM FOR IT

+ THE QUESTIONNAIRE +

Since you're reading this book, you're probably still figuring out which topics you should cover in your essays. As with most writing assignments, the fewer parameters you have, the more difficult it is to begin. However, there's good news: no one is expecting you to churn out a masterpiece in one sitting. The writing process takes time and planning, but getting started is easier than you think.

This questionnaire will help you identify and categorize significant experiences, talents, or interests that will provide great content for your essays. You'll be covering topics such as academic strengths, summer trips, extracurricular activities, and free time. Basically, you're revisiting and itemizing aspects of yourself so it will be easier to see the thematic connections between them and determine which prompt is best suited for you.

As you answer the questions, pay attention to the types of qualities that are conveyed in the story. Ideally, you'll be demonstrating traits such as

+ Patience
+ Dedication
+ Self-discipline
+ Responsibility
+ Creativity
+ Passion
+ Commitment

+ Resourcefulness
+ Intellectual curiosity
+ Selflessness
+ Positive attitude
+ Loyalty

You'll also be looking for opportunities to reveal the angles associated with your student type!

When I help students brainstorm, I always ask them to identify three things about themselves that they want me to know by the time I've finished reading. For example, if coming across as imaginative is your objective, pick an anecdote that illustrates your exceptional creativity. If I can't reflect on your essay by saying something specific—for example, "Oh, he likes to stimulate dialogue on his campus, he makes his classmates laugh, and he's very punctual"—you have written 650 words about something or someone besides, well, you.

QUESTIONNAIRE

It might be helpful to type your answers in a Word document so you can use as much space as you need for your ideas. You may see similarities between this questionnaire and your Common Application forms, although you will be getting a bit more personal here.

1. What is your favorite thing to do on the weekends and why?

2. How did you spend the summer after your freshman year?

3. How did you spend the summer after your sophomore year?

4. How did you spend the summer after your junior year?

5. What are your favorite classes and why?

6. What are your academic weaknesses? Which subjects do you find the most difficult?

7. List all academic clubs you participate in.

	CLUB	NUMBER OF YEARS	LEADERSHIP POSITION(S)
1.			
2.			
3.			

8. List all the sports teams you're a member of.

	SPORTS	NUMBER OF YEARS	LEADERSHIP POSITION(S)
1.			
2.			
3.			

9. List all your non-school-related activities.

10. What is the coolest trip you've ever taken?

11. What's your favorite quote and why?

12. What's your personal philosophy?

13. If you had a free month, how would you spend it?

14. What's a significant problem (on a local, national, or global scale) that you think you could help solve? How would you address it?

15. Do you have any work experience? Describe it.

16. Have you done any community service? Describe it.

17. List three adjectives your friends would use to describe you.

18. Describe an experience in which you felt out of your element.

These answers should be fact based. You'll be analyzing and interpreting them for the freewrite exercise that follows!

CHAPTER 3

GET IT DOWN ON PAPER

+ THE FREEWRITE EXERCISE +

If you think you can just sit down and churn out your magnum opus on your first try, you're in for the rude awakening that I like to call blankly-staring-at-your-computer-and-accomplishing-nothing syndrome. That's why I encourage doing a freewrite, which is by far the most fun step in the essay process. Why? Because you don't have to worry about grammar, spelling, syntax, punctuation. Just use stream-of-consciousness style to get your ideas down on paper. Quickly. Completely. Haphazardly. Look back through your questionnaire and zero in on the ideas that you had the easiest time describing—perhaps because they were the most fun or even just entailed the biggest time commitment. Have you been a leader in a school club or sport for years? Did you take a trip that forced you out of your element? You can pick more than one for now (in fact, pick three or four!), since this is an exercise in generating raw material. Most important, pick items from your questionnaire that you can say a lot about. Write down everything related to those events (people, conversations, emotions, and especially time and place). College essays can easily dissolve into clichéd drivel disguised as analysis, and the only way to save your writing is to tether it to concrete experiences. So you need details. Lots of 'em.

Here are some things to consider as you get started:

1. Try to identify a turning point or precipitous moment that taught you something about yourself. It doesn't have to be

huge, as long as it is meaningful. I have seen successful essays address very somber topics, such as the death of a close friend. I've also seen essays about concocting the perfect fudge brownie recipe, finally beating a sibling in *Dance Dance Revolution*, having a penchant for wearing tie-dye attire, and starting a Wednesday night ironic haiku club that were all well received by top schools. In fact, my favorite essay of all time was on a student's fear of the color red (more on that later). Consider these categories for discussing your questionnaire data:

+ An incident when you had to confront and overcome a fear
+ A moment when you dealt with unexpected failure
+ A conversation that changed your perspective
+ A person who gave you some quirky or sage advice
+ The onset of a hardship
+ Something you are especially proud of
+ A significant loss
+ A change of location
+ A class assignment
+ A scary situation
+ A secret
+ A book that made you view the world differently
+ A problem you haven't yet been able to solve

2. Make it personal. Write about something that happened to you. As I mentioned earlier, do not assume that bigger crises equal better essays; this is unequivocally not the case. Additionally, don't try to create a hardship where none exists. That means if you attend an elite private school, drive a BMW, and have multiple summer homes, don't write about how the economic recession has affected you. I have seen students give this approach a shot—one student went on and on about how difficult it was for her to find a job, so she had to take a luxury safari instead. You can guess what happened to that draft.

3. Look at your questionnaire and flesh things out!

Here's an example of a great, lengthy freewrite. Following protocol, this part-Achieve-o-Tron, part-Aristocrat student (whom we'll call Sarah) did not worry about grammar or spelling at this stage. While filling out her questionnaire, she noticed that she had the most material about figure skating, a recent trip to Egypt, and an independent research project on sustainable fashion manufacturing. Because she is an Achieve-o-Tron, she wanted to discuss not accomplishments but rather events that had challenged her, and because of her Aristocrat status, she had to be careful about how she presented her vacation to Egypt. So, she started describing (take a deep breath—it's *long*):

> Traveling to Egypt was an experience, somewhat frightening but somewhat exciting. Frightening was getting off at Heathrow all alone, being stopped at immigration for not having parental permission to enter the UK, finding my connecting flight and having a 7 hour wait, and landing in a foreign country with no Americans in sight at 2 a.m. When I got off the plane in Cairo, I had no idea what to expect. There were no Americans around and it was somewhat difficult to communicate. I am sure people spoke English but no one was doing it this morning. The airport was filthy and dark, unlike the British Airways terminal I left in London, and I had to figure out how to buy my $15 Visa. I then had to go through customs alone and really didn't know which gate I was supposed to go through. They were taking pictures of everyone when they walk through, which was confusing to me as to why they needed a picture of everyone coming into the country. I imagine that is part of their Homeland Security. When I finally met up with my friend, it was around 3 in the morning and I was pretty tired and overwhelmed by everything around me. We hopped into her car and her driver drove for about 30 minutes to her home. One of the first sights I remember seeing was the Nile river (along with some garbage lining the edge). After all the ancient Egyptian history that I studied, to drive past the Nile river, was just phenomenal.

I guess I can talk about the contrast and contradictions of what I saw in Cairo.

In many ways, Cairo is like any large modern western city. My friend and I went to the gym to work out and ate sushi at night. However, then there were the children on the streets begging for money. In many cases these children were alone and in some cases I saw their parents sending the kids up to you for money. It was heartbreaking.

Cairo was unbelievable. Living among the sights, sounds, and unique customs of the exotic city, and the pyramids, the camels, the friends I made. I was somewhat surprised to see KFC and Pizza Hut.

I saw men riding camels, as well as donkeys.

Shopping in Egypt requires a lot of effort. When purchasing something, you bargained with the owner, ask them for the price, offer about half of it, then they laugh at you, so you offer a little bit more. They say no, and you walk out, as you are walking out, they say no no no okay fine, thinking they are doing you a favor. It was really fun to negotiate for prices.

Egypt was a beautiful place and full of culture and history. Looking at the small details as well as the larger picture can give you a better idea of the history. I still can't get over how every block on the Pyramids was placed there by a man, thousands of years ago. Standing on the pyramids in Giza, you just can't get over just how large every block actually is. The temples, now worn down and dirty, used to be full of color, riches, and hieroglyphs.

Being female in Egypt you are treated very differently than back home. When leaving the Pyramids, a camel driver approached my friend and I and offered 20 camels for my hand in marriage. My response, I'm worth more than 20 camels, and walked away.

But then I want to bring it back into what I am interested in—"the business of fashion."

I want to take my experience in Egypt and what I saw with all the street children and somehow lead this into my independent study project this semester on sustainability in the US fashion industry. It is not just about the environmental impact of the industry but also the ethical and social impact. Society looks the other way to the problems of child labor and sweatshops. I believe that US Fashion companies need to be better citizens of the world and take serious their social responsibility to eliminate these horrible conditions that children are working under. This will not solve the problems of the children of Cairo, but in some other country, it just may improve a child's life.

Although I enjoy fashion, I believe it is our moral obligation to ensure that humane standards are upheld in the production of fashion garments. Even in pursuing a career in fashion, which doesn't sound very humanitarian, I can do something really something to benefit society. I don't have to join the Peace Corps, be a doctor or social worker to actually make a difference. I can actually pursue my passion and still do some good.

The elimination of sweatshops and child labor requires the cooperation of the US fashion industry, and as I have seen the horrible conditions that the street children in Cairo live under, I want to be one of the future leaders of the fashion world who realize that human rights and profits can work together. My independent study is meant to increase exposure. (This may sound too much like Mother Teresa, so I have to say it better.)

I am an independent thinker and I come up with original ideas that I want to pursue. I may not be a leader of any group, but still consider myself a leader because I follow my own ideas and people seem to want to follow me in that way. Leadership isn't just being the President of a school club, but it could also be shown through coming up with your own ideas and pursuing them. I am definitely not a follower, so therefore I must be a leader.

I was thinking about discussing Emerson and his theme of becoming a self-reliant individual. When I read Emerson, I thought of how I actually was following his teachings. He talked about breaking through the social and self-imposed barriers that limit one's individuality, and that is somewhat like what I did when I went to France, Egypt, and my junior year course selection. One of Emerson's big lessons was to "trust thyself." I always had my own unique thoughts and I followed them.

I think I have a good idea of what I want to do with my life and what I want to pursue it with all my passion.

It all started at 4 years old, when I was watching some skating competition and told my parents that's what I wanted to do. For the next 10 years, I trained, fell a lot, injured numerous muscles on different parts of my body, woke up at 6 a.m. to skate before school, froze, fell some more, competed, won gold, silver and bronze, lost and even threw up on the ice during a test, and finally figured out that I was not going to be Sarah Hughes and realized the sacrifice to try was just not worth it (as my Micro Economics teacher would say, I did a marginal cost, marginal benefit analysis and the marginal cost was much higher than the marginal benefit, so it was time to stop) Knowing when to stop is not quitting.

Freshman–Sophomore year, I wanted to spend a summer in Paris. No one in my grade went that early. Now that is another story. Thought I would learn about other cultures. Big lesson that summer was a test of my ethics as my roommate was out of control and the house I was living in really had no parental supervision. (Maybe one theme is that the biggest lessons are those that you don't expect.)

Junior year—no other girl did this one—AP Stats, Honors Physics, Pre-Calc. For someone who is really not interested in a career in science or engineering, that threesome was off the wall. There was a time in Honors Physics that I had the highest grade in the class and it really pissed off one of the brains in the class. I really got a kick out of that. Physics was ok for me. As the course progressed, it got somewhat rough, but I was able to come out with a B+. Teacher was a female, which I admired.

Not all freewrites are this thorough, but you can definitely see that once you begin typing, the ideas will flow. Sarah discusses topics she wants to cover and comparisons she wants to make, which will help her organize by theme. She will have to eliminate most of these ideas, but that isn't a bad thing; with this much raw material at her disposal, she will have an easy time selecting the best details to include. Once she is finished, every single sentence of the essay will contribute to the overall meaning. She won't have to use any filler to make sure she hits the appropriate word count, and that makes for a cleaner, more poignant personal statement.

CHAPTER 4

MAKE IT COUNT

+ CHOOSING THE BEST PROMPT FOR YOU +

Prior to August 2013, the "choose your own topic" prompt was in full force, so students didn't really have to consider the fine points of answering a specific question. Ah, freedom. Unfortunately, the updated Common Application cut this option, leaving you with five specific, and required, ways of framing your 650-word personal statement. Many students tackled this new challenge by starting with the prompts, selecting a particular question, then brainstorming a story that clearly and directly answered it.

I disagree with this approach. To me, it makes more sense to take inventory of your material and then see which prompt allows you to discuss the experiences and traits you've chosen to illustrate. That is why I wanted you to read this chapter not right off the bat, but after you'd done your freewrite. If you have a particular prompt in mind when you're getting everything down on paper, you might accidentally leave out interesting details—or worse, tell a snooze-inducing anecdote!

Now that you've identified your student type and gathered the raw material for your essay, you're ready to take a closer look at your five options.

PROMPT #1

Some students have a background or story that is so central to their identity that they believe their application would be incomplete without it. If this sounds like you, then please share your story.

This prompt is great for

+ Club Presidents who want to give insight into their character and show that they are more than just a litany of organizations and titles
+ Buddies who want to highlight their outgoing personalities
+ Achieve-o-Trons who want to add a little oomph to their application

This prompt is iffy for

- Dabblers who really need to focus on more recent interests and experiences
- Aristocrats who might accidentally sound snobby by discussing their privileged backgrounds

PROMPT #2

Recount an incident or time when you experienced failure. How did it affect you, and what lessons did you learn?

This prompt is great for

+ Achieve-o-Trons who need to show a little humility
+ Naturals who want to prove that they can put in effort
+ Buddies whose strength is their buoyancy
+ Un-Naturals whose strength is their doggedness

This prompt is iffy for

- Dabblers who need to demonstrate successes
- Aristocrats for whom failure might be manufactured or embellished

PROMPT #3

Reflect on a time when you challenged a belief or idea. What prompted you to act? Would you make the same decision again?

This prompt is great for

+ Aristocrats who want to take the focus off their backgrounds and flex a little mental muscle
+ Athletes who want to showcase their cerebral sides
+ Naturals who need to show that not everything comes easily to them
+ Dabblers who want to show dedication
+ Average Joes who want to take up a cause

This prompt is iffy for

Eh, no one. This is my favorite prompt. It's a great lead-in for showing what makes you tick!

PROMPT #4

Describe a place or environment where you are perfectly content. What do you do or experience there, and why is it meaningful to you?

This prompt is great for

+ Secret Prodigies who need to explain how they spend their free time
+ Average Joes who want to describe a true passion or newfound interest
+ Un-Naturals who want to prove that they are motivated by more than just grades
+ Dabblers who need to discuss a long-standing hobby
+ Buddies who want to portray themselves in their natural states: easily interacting with and befriending others

This prompt is iffy for

- Achieve-o-Trons who could get carried away with tooting their own horns
- Naturals who presumably feel at ease everywhere

PROMPT #5

Discuss an accomplishment or event, formal or informal, that marked your transition from childhood to adulthood within your culture, community, or family.

This prompt is great for

+ Athletes who want to explore why a sport has been important—and/or relate it to an academic feat
+ Secret Prodigies who need to explain the profound significance of their independent endeavors
+ Club Presidents who want to reveal a side that doesn't show up on their transcripts

This prompt is iffy for

- Average Joes who need a more intellectual, less emotional topic

These pointers are meant to help guide you, not to compel you to rule out choices. Do not feel discouraged if you are a Dabbler who wants to discuss a failure; it might not be your best option, but hey, you can make anything work if you keep your student type in mind as you craft your essay. Remember: start by assessing your freewrite material, and then pick a prompt!

CHAPTER 5

ORGANIZE IT

+ THE OUTLINE +

Now that you've picked a prompt, you're ready to begin organizing your essay based on the angles and imperatives of your student type. As I explained earlier, you are not pigeonholing yourself with this type of classification; rather, you are making it easier for admissions officers to really connect with your application. If they can't get a clear idea of who you are and what you'd contribute to their school, you're not getting in. You might still be exploring and developing your identity in real life, but the voice of your essay needs to be confident, insightful, and focused.

Let's return to Sarah. After analyzing the themes of her free-write and wanting to show her ability to make the best of situations that did not go as planned, she came up with the following options for her essay:

1. Prompt #2 (failure). Catering to her Achieve-o-Tron imperative, she could discuss how moving on from figure skating allowed her to indulge her adventurous side through travel.

2. Prompt #3 (challenging a belief or idea). She understands that expectations and reality don't always coincide. This topic relates to her experience in Paris (with regard to her roommate), as well as her trip to Egypt (as there was a stark contrast between what she'd studied in history class and present-day Cairo).

3. Prompt #3 (challenging a belief or idea). She wants to change the questionable side of the fashion industry and show how clothes can be ethically manufactured. This would allow her to discuss her project on sustainable fashion.

4. Prompt #1 (central story). Sarah could discuss both her trip to Egypt and her fashion project—topics that touch upon her adventurous side and independence and help give her intellectual pursuits a bit more direction.

The last topic is the strongest choice because it would allow Sarah to discuss multiple episodes from her life. It also relates to the way she views and interprets her experiences, implying that she's open to new ideas and creative, interdisciplinary approaches to learning. Since her transcript will attest to her many achievements, it is good for Sarah to demonstrate the type of thinker she is: she strives to devise practical solutions using her own strengths, which shows that she wants to incite actual change, not just identify huge, pervasive problems. With this option, Sarah could say the most about herself.

So Sarah moves forward with option # 4. As you read through the outline she concocted, keep in mind that, while beautiful and thorough, it is also quite lengthy and ambitious. Sarah will get a better idea of what can reasonably fit within the word count once she begins writing, but for now this structure will help her put ideas down on paper. As with the freewrite exercise, it is easier to cut material than to add it after the fact.

I. Introduction:

a. Although I consider myself to be an adventurous person, I had never really traveled outside of the country before [aside from a chaperoned summer program in Paris]

b. After a figure skating injury, I needed to find another outlet for my adventurous side

II. I had the opportunity to a visit family friend in Egypt— [to avoid sounding too much like an "Aristocrat," I must stress the intellectual nature of this trip]

a. What I was expecting—one sentence [perhaps—sweeping panoramas of sand punctuated by pyramids]

b. How nothing could have prepared me for the reality of the experience

    i. The whole ordeal of getting there

    ii. The taxi drivers [the traffic lights were a suggestion rather than an imperative]

    iii. Litter and flashy party boats in the Nile River—the jarring juxtaposition of sacrosanct history [the Nile I had studied in my ancient history classes] and modern poverty [I want to use this metaphor—the idea of something vs. the reality of the situation. I tried to reconcile these contradictions during my trip]

III. Other experiences/insights from Egypt—this is where I should give some analysis

a. A man offers camels for my hand in marriage—catcalls on the street [I shouldn't make any generalizations about women in this society, but I can possibly show disparities in treatment between the sexes through my own observations]

b. However, even with the modern conveniences and massive pyramids on the horizon, it's hard to overlook the rampant poverty [and children living among the garbage]—be descriptive

c. When I return—everyone asks about the Pyramids—that is all people really know about Egypt. I tried to explain that these structures are just steps from the city [not out in the middle of the desert as they are often pictured] and across the street from a pizza hut and KFC.

IV. Fashion and Emerson tie-ins

a. This trip gave momentum to my independent study project on sustainability in the US fashion industry—again, I can show the contradiction between idea and reality [the glamour, beauty, and celebrity of the fashion industry vs. the unethical ways in which the clothes are sometimes manufactured]

b. It is not just about the environmental impact of the industry but also the ethical and social impact. Society looks the other way when it comes to the problems of child labor and sweatshops. I believe that US Fashion companies need to be better citizens of the world and be serious about their social responsibility to eliminate these horrible conditions inflicted on children. This may not solve the problems of child poverty in Cairo, but in some other country, it just may improve a child's life. A small gesture often inspires systemic change—I wanted my project to have redemptive social value. Behind the historical significance and sensory overload of Cairo are the kind, incredibly friendly people.

V. Concluding ideas

a. One of Emerson's central doctrines in his essays on self-reliance is "trust thyself"—this has always been my personal mantra.

b. I cannot wait to travel again—I relish being immersed in a culture so entirely different from my own. The best ideas arise when I am out of my comfort zone, interacting with new people on my own [when I discuss my observations from my trip, I shouldn't spend too much time on my travel companions—although being with people from different backgrounds is interesting, it would take me on an unrelated trajectory about tolerance and finding common ground, and then my essay would lack thematic cohesion].

c. The most important lessons are often the least expected ones, but they always start with people.

For now, this flow of ideas will help Sarah write a detailed, albeit too long, first draft. On that note, it's time to make grammar and punctuation a priority once again!

CHAPTER 6

WHEN TO USE "IT'S"

+ THE SKINNY ON CONTRACTIONS +

Every year, without fail, parents call me in a panic because the essays their children have been working on contain gasp-inducing informal constructions such as "can't," "don't," and "wouldn't." They want to know whether these contractions are acceptable, since their gut tells them that this is a formal piece of writing and should be treated as such. As with every issue related to college applications, each person you ask will give you a different answer, some closer to the mark than others. Here's what I've learned from my experience: contractions are never a deal breaker. No doubt you have had English teachers who hated them and penalized you for using them in your *Scarlet Letter* essays, as well as teachers who didn't care one way or the other. Each fall you had to learn, and cater to, a new teacher's preferences and demands for how an essay should look; but when it comes to your applications, colleges just want you to sound like yourself. In this book I repeatedly warn you to avoid putting on airs. You are a teenager with a unique viewpoint and distinct experiences, so channel that, and only that, identity. However, there is a thin line between sounding authentic and coming off as flippant or lazy, so make sure your tone isn't overly casual. Here are some tips to keep in mind.

NOT ALL CONTRACTIONS ARE
CREATED EQUAL

In general, I tell students that a few of the "not" contractions are so common and familiar that they will be fairly innocuous in their essays. That list includes

Can't

Couldn't

Won't

Wouldn't

Isn't

Aren't

Don't

Doesn't

Didn't

Hasn't

Haven't

Hadn't

Wasn't

Weren't

Additionally, pronoun contractions involving I, you, he, she, it, we, and they can be acceptable.

I'll

I've

You'll

You've

He's

She's

It's

They're

We're

Notice how I left out certain varieties of these forms, such as "I'd," "you'd," "he'd," "she'd," and "they'd." Present tense contractions (those involving "is") and present perfect tense contractions (those involving "has" and "have") are safer than those with "had." Go ahead and show admissions officers that you've mastered the past perfect tense. While you're at it, take an extra second to write out your "could," "would," and "should" phrases, since "I could have given up" or "They would rather go" are preferable to "I could've given up" and "They'd rather go."

On that note, the "have" contractions almost always sound awkward and forced in a personal statement. Try to stay away from

Might've
Must've
Would've
Could've
Should've

Don't use the "who," "what," "when," "where," "why," and "how" contractions unless context absolutely necessitates them. That list includes

Who'll
Who'd
Who's
What'll
What'd
When'll
When's
When'd
Where'll
Where's
Where'd

Why'll

Why's

Why'd

How'll

How'd

The exceptions here are "what's" and "how's," which can fit if you're incorporating dialogue.

Never ever use "y'all" or "ain't."

CHARACTER RESTRICTIONS CAN MAKE CONTRACTIONS NECESSARY

While you will have reasonable space for your personal statement, as well as for some supplements that limit you to paragraphs, not characters or words (thank you, University of Chicago, for the leeway!), you will inevitably have to write at least one response restricted to 175, 300, 1,000, or 1,500 characters. In those instances, getting your message across trumps formality, so admissions officers will read your writing with those space constraints in mind. Brown, for instance, often asks you to explain in 250 characters where you have lived and for how long, so "I've spent the past five years in Morristown, NJ" makes more sense than spelling out every word, particularly the state. For Yale's 175-character short takes, you'll definitely want to use "I'd" when you explain the historical event you wish you could have witnessed firsthand.

CONSIDER YOUR VOICE

If a formal construction makes you sound like you're playing dress-up in a tweed blazer with suede elbow patches instead of expressing your distinct, authentic voice, change it.

CONSIDER THE VOICES OF OTHERS

If it's dialogue, write the way someone would talk, to an extent.

There is a time and a place for slang if it makes sense in context or, more commonly, appears in dialogue, but use it sparingly. A good rule of thumb is, if certain elements of your writing— repeated words, monotonous sentence structure, unnatural vocabulary, and so on—draw attention to themselves, change them. You want the focus on your message, not the way it is packaged. If you read all that and are still frantic about the "wouldn't" in your third paragraph, see if anyone else gets tripped up by it. If it passes unnoticed, you're in the clear. The bottom line, though, is this: don't overthink it.

CHAPTER 7

TIDY IT UP

+ THE DRAFT +

You're probably dying to see how Sarah's essay turned out. Here's one of her earlier drafts:

When I was in ninth grade, I found myself sprawled out on a glossy ice rink after attempting a double combination jump during a regional competition; my tights were torn, my hip was bruised, and my palm was cold and red from breaking my fall. After ten years of skating competitively, I had weighed the costs and benefits of pursuing this sport and already understood that it was time to move on. However, I knew I would miss the exhilaration of speeding across the rink and leaping into the air, whether I ultimately landed the jump or fell before a stadium of spectators. It was the challenge that held me in thrall, rather than skating itself, and I decided to find a new outlet for my daring side. I immediately set my sights on traveling because in my sixteen years, I hadn't once ventured outside the country. A summer program in Paris after my sophomore year amplified this desire to explore, and last July, I got a taste of the adventure I had been seeking when I found myself arriving in Cairo at 2 a.m.

My structured, chaperoned, academic program in the City of Light had in no way prepared me for the sensory overload of Cairo; the chaos was charming in its own way, but I found it utterly disorienting after almost 24 hours of flights and layovers. I changed my money to Egyptian pounds and somehow figured out how to buy my visa at a side window, then joined the amorphous crowd that was funneling, with no apparent order, past the customs booths. Unfortunately, the fact that I was sixteen, female, and alone attracted suspicious attention from the customs officials, and I was singled out for additional questioning. I finally located my friend at baggage claim, and as we ate a very late dinner back at her apartment, I could hear the broadcasted call to prayer echoing off every surface of the city. I was in the Middle East, and I couldn't have been more excited.

Looking back on my month in Egypt, I was struck by the disparity between my expectations and my actual experience. The Nile I had studied in history class was littered with neon party boats blasting electronic music, and the pyramids were situated near a Pizza Hut and a KFC rather than, as I had always imagined, expanses of sun-drenched sand. I was also struck by the number of unfinished buildings I saw along the monochromatic skyline, and soon learned that construction was commonly stopped early to avoid the 10 percent tax imposed on all finished buildings. Venturing out into the markets, my friend and I always made sure our limbs were fully covered, but this didn't stop various merchants from offering us camels for our hands in marriage. The soot, heat, and sweat were overwhelming at times, yet I relished them. The Egyptians were some of the friendliest people I have ever met, and I loved how heckling over the price of a scarf could result in a two-hour conversation about our families. The only aspect of Cairo that haunted rather than fascinated me was the rampant poverty, and while my Egyptian friend was accustomed to the emaciated children scampering among piles of garbage, I simply could not look away. There are many areas of the United States that suffer from destitution, but in Cairo, the problem seemed more pervasive.

"This is terrible," I muttered to my friend as a child approached us, hand outstretched.

"You have no idea," she replied.

When I arrived home, everyone asked about the pyramids, the Sphinx, the Nile. However, there was more to explain, as I was still trying to reconcile the contradictions between the idea of Egypt and the reality that I had seen. In an unexpected way, this jarring juxtaposition of sacrosanct history and modern poverty inspired my independent study this semester. My project focuses on sustainability in the U.S. fashion industry, and examines more than just the environmental impact; it delves into the social and ethical consequences as well. The glamour, beauty, and celebrity of the fashion industry often stand in stark contrast to the unethical ways in which clothes are manufactured. I hope to enforce responsibility rather than simply encourage it. It is critical for the fashion industry to not only maintain certain core principles, such as fair wages and safe working conditions, but also cease the exploitation of women in third-world countries. Most importantly, child labor must be eradicated. After my trip to Cairo, I knew I wanted to design a project that had redemptive social value and that forced industries to consider their global operations on a human level. Over the past few years, I've transferred my time and energy from skating to a project I find equally exciting but infinitely more rewarding.

This is a great first effort: thorough, grammatically correct, filled with sophisticated vocabulary words, and extremely thoughtful. Unfortunately, it has a few negative qualities as well:

1. The word count is over 800, which is prohibitively long.

2. While the figure skating incident sheds light on Sarah's character, it isn't the strongest way to start an essay on sustainable fashion. It makes it seem as if Sarah quit figure skating because of a particular fall, not because she analyzed the costs and benefits of pursuing the sport and opted to pour her energy into a new endeavor. The only narrative thread tying this episode to the other paragraphs is an insight into her sense of adventure, and readers can pick up on this even without the opening paragraph. Perhaps the most important

argument against the inclusion of this paragraph is the fact that the figure skating material is better suited for an activity essay if any of her supplements calls for one.

3. The final paragraph, in which Sarah discusses the significant independent project she has initiated, seems rushed. Rather than simply giving an overview of the philosophy and observations behind her project, Sarah needs to explain what actions she is taking to make a difference. Meetings with executives in the fashion industry, for instance, would be an impressive addition to her discussion. Of course, one cannot fake that, so she should probably make some phone calls first!

4. The connection between the trip to Egypt and the senior project is a bit tenuous, so Sarah needs to draw stronger parallels. She might help solidify the link by including an observation about child labor, rather than simply recounting the poverty.

With this feedback in mind, here's how Sarah revised her draft:

My eyes were glued to the oval window as my flight landed in Cairo at 2 a.m. I had jumped at the opportunity to spend a month visiting my friend Salema in Egypt, but I had no idea just how much I would gain from being in this utterly different environment.

Nothing could have prepared me for the sensory overload of Cairo, which I found fascinating but disorienting after almost 24 hours of travel. Being alone, sixteen, and female, I attracted attention from the customs officials, and I was singled out for additional questioning. Frightened, I explained that I was visiting my childhood neighbor, whose family had moved back to Cairo. I finally located Salema at baggage claim, and as we arrived at her home around 5 a.m., I was captivated by the serenading calls to prayer.

Looking back on my month in Egypt, I am struck by the disparity between my expectations and my actual experience. The Nile I had studied was littered with neon party boats blasting electronic music. The pyramids were situated near a Pizza Hut rather than, as I had always imagined, expanses of sun-drenched sand. Venturing out into the markets, we were respectful and made sure our limbs were fully covered. This didn't stop one street vendor from offering 20 camels for my hand in marriage. I politely responded, "I am worth more than that." The soot and heat were overwhelming at times, yet I savored them. The Egyptian people were some of the friendliest I have ever met, and I loved how haggling over the price of a scarf for my sister turned into a two-hour conversation about our families. The only aspect of Cairo that haunted rather than intrigued me was the rampant poverty, and while my Egyptian friend was accustomed to the emaciated children, I simply could not look away. These small figures, lost among the crowds in the city, seemed invisible and ignored.

"This is terrible," I whispered to Salema as a child approached us, hand outstretched. "You have no idea," she replied. I later discovered that it was common for kids as young as five to work in local factories, weaving clothes or tanning leather. In fact, the Egyptian cotton sold in the United States is usually picked by children working in the fields.

When I arrived home, everyone asked about the pyramids, the Sphinx, and the Nile. However, there was more to explain, as I was still trying to reconcile the contradictions between the idea of Egypt and the reality that I had seen. Interestingly, this juxtaposition of sacrosanct history and modern poverty inspired my independent study this semester. My project focuses on sustainability in the U.S. fashion industry and examines more than just the environmental impact; it delves into the social and ethical consequences as well. I am exploring how the glamour and celebrity of the fashion industry often stand in stark contrast to the unethical manufacturing methods. I know that much of poverty is caused by injustice, and solutions require economic, social, and structural change, so I intend to show how the U.S. fashion industry has the power and obligation to ensure that their products are produced under safe, legal, and humane working conditions. After my trip to Cairo, I knew I wanted to design a project that had redemptive social value, and raising awareness about these issues is my way of inciting change. I'm even speaking with representatives from various fashion companies, such as Ralph Lauren, to learn about their corporate social responsibility practices.

I'm someone who strives to find connections between seemingly different people, places, or disciplines. Thus, I can't wait to see where this project will lead and what my next travel adventure might inspire.

This version shows how the same ideas can become more convincing if they are presented differently. Eliminating the information about ice-skating makes the piece seem more cohesive, and ending with a discussion of her learning style shows admissions committees that Sarah evinces tremendous intellectual potential. Additionally, the brief but powerful dialogue about child exploitation helps her transition to a promotion of fair labor practices. Beautifully written, thorough, and mature, this essay is the perfect foundation for a college application.

Not everyone is lucky enough to have traveled extensively or pursued independent research, however, so the next chapter will show how even common topics can stand out if discussed from the right angle. More often than not, it is not the subject of your essay, but rather, your perspective on that subject, that will give you an advantage in the admissions game.

By the way, Sarah was accepted, early decision, to her first-choice top-tier school.

CHAPTER 8

MAKE IT UNIQUE

+ YOUR VERSION OF THE MOST COMMON LONG ESSAYS +

For this section, I took inventory of many of the students I've helped in the past, as well as the essay topics they attempted to tackle. I changed names but kept characteristics, circumstances, and choices intact so that it is easy to see the essay process in action. These topics are the most popular when it comes to the Common Application personal statement, yet my goal is to show you that [*drum roll*]

1. Anyone can successfully write about anything.

2. Even a predictable subject can be tackled in a fresh, engaging way.

THE SPORTS ESSAY

Good for addressing Common Application prompts #1 (background story), #2 (experience with failure), #4 (place where you feel content), and #5 (transition to adulthood).

STUDENT 1: SCOTT (ATHLETE, AVERAGE JOE)

Scott is an average student, a favorite among his teachers for his endearing, positive attitude and earnest efforts in class, but he is never one to ace tests without studying or to participate in academically based extracurricular activities. His father is a sports fanatic, having played both football and soccer at a Division I school, and he has fervently encouraged Scott's athletic interests for years. As a result, Scott spends the majority of his nonclass time at practice, playing for both his school's soccer team and an elite club team that has weekend games all over the country. He normally spends half of his summer at selective skills camps and the other half coaching local elementary-school teams at the community park. Posters of famous soccer players, such as Pelé, Ronaldinho, and David Beckham, line his bedroom walls, and every morning when he arrives on campus he dribbles a ball from the school parking lot to the upper school building.

Despite this, Scott is not the best player on either of his soccer teams. He has been constantly playing for so many years that he's developed polished techniques, but his playing instincts during games are only average. He sometimes wonders whether he would have pursued soccer so aggressively if not for the influence of his dad, but the sport has been such a huge part of his life that he can't comprehend his personality or identity without it. His parents have put pressure on him to earn a spot at a top-tier school and play throughout college, but Scott frequently worries that he won't live up to their expectations, or that he'll simply burn out.

Last season, Scott was sidelined for a few months because of acute shin splints, and though it was initially frustrating to be on the bench and out of the action, he soon began to appreciate the downtime. He was present for every practice and game on his schedule, traveled with both teams, and offered encouragement and support to his friends when necessary. Eventually he became truly grateful for his injury because it allowed him to experience all the aspects of soccer he truly loved, from the team dynamic and camaraderie to the sportsmanship and excitement, without the parts he disliked, such as competition among teammates, intense pressure, and anxiety about mistakes. Because of his dedication, he was elected captain by his teammates for the following year.

When planning his college essays, Scott didn't have much trouble choosing a topic. In fact, since he'd devoted all his energy to soccer, he didn't really have a choice; no other activity meant as much to him or monopolized as much of his time. Scott defined himself by his devotion to soccer and figured that admissions officers could learn the most about him through a discussion of the sport. In short, he felt that the soccer field was his second home, and he wanted to convey that point.

What's GOOD About Scott's Thinking?

Scott is in a tough position. To focus on anything besides soccer would be a mistake, because he wouldn't have enough to say, but at the same time he doesn't want to seem like a one-trick pony. Admissions officers will look at Scott's transcript and see very few extracurricular activities, so it's important for him to explain the extreme dedication and time commitment his soccer career has required. This is a chance for Scott to discuss something he enjoys and *knows*.

What's BAD About Scott's Thinking?

As mentioned before, it's always dangerous to seem one-dimensional. The last thing Scott wants admissions officers to say is, "Okay, so he plays soccer, but what will he be like in the classroom?" The essay is a chance to tell admissions committees something unique about yourself that they cannot learn from the other parts of your application. If Scott were to take this route, he should definitely not ask either of his coaches for a letter of recommendation; instead, he should approach one of his other teachers who can attest to his academic potential, not just his sports career. Additionally, because he is an Athlete student type, he really needs to show some mental, not just athletic, power, and his Average Joe side needs to demonstrate a growing passion for something unexpected.

The Essay

Let's assume Scott sticks to his plan and writes the essay. Even though there are obvious pitfalls, this is still Scott's strongest topic option. To make the essay seem fresh and interesting, however, he needs to include the following points and techniques.

1. Scott needs to begin with an anecdote that shows how he is using his athletic side to make strides in the classroom. For instance, he can describe the moment in physics class when he easily grasped, and then helped his classmates to visualize, the conservation of momentum in the Magnus Effect by putting topspin on a soccer kick; or how, in his Latin American politics elective, he gave a presentation on Argentine leaders who formerly headed up some of the country's most high-profile football clubs. Regardless of the specifics, the point here is that soccer is significant to Scott not only on the field but also in school, where it provides an unexpected catalyst for interpretation and insight.

2. From there, Scott can reflect on how the sport became such a significant part of his life: when he first started playing, when he got his first soccer ball as a birthday present, his first team (the Yellow Jackets). He needs to mention his father's athletic past, and how much his parents encouraged not just his interest in the sport but also his talent for it.

3. Now Scott can discuss how the activity snowballed into daily practices, summer camps, and away games, and in the process became something he did rather than something he loved. He needs to express his doubts about whether his energy should have been channeled elsewhere.

4. The injury and its aftermath: an exasperating event becomes a blessing in disguise as Scott remembers what he loved about soccer and realizes it's been his passion, not just his lifestyle, all along; it's not simply something his father chose for him but something Scott continued to choose, year after year, for himself. His teammates rewarded him for his attitude and perseverance by electing him captain, and he got a second wind.

5. Scott needs to describe the next steps: how he intends to play in college, not because his parents expect it but because he finds the team companionship and solidarity enriching. This is also an opportunity to mention other interests he'd like to explore: graphic design, chemistry, perhaps even computer programming. He can reference the intellectual example from

the first paragraph as well, since it shows that soccer gives him so much more than just an athletic or social outlet. This is where Scott's cerebral side *must* be reinforced.

Why this approach works:

- + It assures readers that Scott's commitment to soccer has made him more, not less, engaged in the classroom.
- + It confirms his love of soccer and illustrates the importance of the experience.
- + It shows that Scott had the maturity to express self-doubt and undergo self-evaluation, and that he came out on the other end even surer of his commitment.
- + He mentions other interests he wants to pursue in college, which shows that he's going to be an active member of his campus community and he's interested in trying new things.
- + It addresses potential admissions committee concerns that soccer might prevent him from doing anything else. Scott explicitly states that his team would give him comfort, stability, routine, and friendship, and that it would also serve as a launching pad for other endeavors.

How the essay could fail:

- – If Scott mentions how his father got him excited about soccer without explaining why or how Scott came to truly love it himself, the admissions committees would worry that he hadn't had a chance to pursue his own interests, and that as a result his dedication to soccer would invariably wane.
- – If Scott omits the academic example in the opening paragraph, the essay may seem clichéd and one-dimensional. He has to do more with this sport than just score goals. Moreover, if Scott doesn't end the essay by expressing interest in other activities, admissions committees may wonder whether he could contribute anything interesting to their campus, or even if he'd bother to get involved in the wide variety of courses and clubs offered in college.

STUDENT 2: CAROLINE (ATHLETE, ACHIEVE-O-TRON)

Caroline, like Scott, is a well-liked student who has been play-ing sports her entire life; however, that's where the similarities end. Her parents are both scientists, and her mom even helps write computer programs for NASA. Neither parent is very ath-letic, so Caroline's interest in tennis hadn't been initiated by an outside force. She simply picked up a tennis racket during her fourth grade physical education class and aced an overhand serve on her first try, astonishing both her coaches and her classmates. Caroline's parents agreed to let her take lessons and compete in tournaments as long as academics continued to be her main priority, and over the years she maintained impressive national rankings in the sport. She was the Most Valuable Player and cap-tain of her school's tennis team, and everyone assumed her track record and rare natural ability would earn her a spot on a Divi-sion I college team.

Right after her sixteenth birthday, though, Caroline was involved in a car accident and shattered her right arm, rendering her unable to play tennis while it healed. She was devastated, not only because she'd have to miss her season but also because her rankings would drop due to her absence from tournaments. Moreover, she was concerned that even when her arm recovered, her muscles would have atrophied from months in the cast and she'd be seriously out of practice. For weeks, she wondered if she'd ever be able to play at such a high level again.

Always a self-starter and optimist, Caroline finally snapped out of her disappointed state and began to pursue other interests that up until that point had never fit into her busy schedule. She joined the school choir and a student-run a cappella group, sing-ing first alto at weekend concerts. She also spent her free evenings working as a research assistant for her dad, a psychology pro-fessor who was conducting a study on the way different smells trigger memories. Caroline focused on her schoolwork and main-tained stellar grades, and she diligently practiced writing with her left hand so she could keep up with her class note taking. Overall, she discovered that she was adept at quite a few things, from singing and painting to science and math.

Caroline continued to be an active member of her tennis team, attending practices to offer suggestions and support, and helping the coach manage the schedule and roster. She truly missed tennis, but she grew confident that she'd be able to play again once her arm recovered, and besides, her self-esteem had received a great boost from her newly discovered talents in other areas. Despite the injury and her diverse interests, though, Caroline still wanted to write a college essay about how important tennis was to her.

What's GOOD About Caroline's Thinking?

Caroline is in the best possible position; not only does she have a thorough understanding of tennis, but she also has a sincere interest in the sport, as well as extremely promising talent. As soccer was for Scott, Caroline's sport has required so much time, energy, and commitment that it's become an essential aspect of her identity. She clearly has a lot of material, and through tennis she can discuss many of her personal qualities that would impress any admissions committee: dedication, self-discipline, ability, and passion.

What's BAD About Caroline's Thinking?

While it's smart for Caroline to discuss her love of tennis, she'd be doing herself a disservice to discuss *only* this subject, because she's clearly good at many other things. She doesn't want to pigeonhole herself as a tennis player when an admissions officer might be seeking a tennis-playing singer or scientist.

The Essay

Let's assume Caroline ultimately picks this topic for her essay. Even though the sports theme is perfect for students such as Caroline, she still needs to be careful when presenting her ideas so she doesn't appear one-dimensional. Here's how she should proceed:

1. Caroline should open with a present-tense narrative in the middle of a heated match. Here she should show her expertise, not by bragging but by using specific tennis terms and by building suspense. Instead of ending with a match-winning point or a successful cross-court backhand shot, however,

she should pick a humbling moment in which she lost or faltered, and thus subvert the reader's expectations. This disappointment is a good way to transition from the court to a season-ending injury.

2. Caroline should briefly discuss the aftermath of the car accident and her shattered forearm. Here she can reflect on tennis as her most important extracurricular activity: her unexpected introduction to the sport during elementary-school gym class, how she had a mature discussion with her parents and took the initiative to hone her skills, and how it was always something she loved—not something anyone pressured her to pursue.

3. Now Caroline needs to launch into a discussion about her post-injury attitude adjustment. She had been exclusively playing tennis for so long that she hadn't fully explored other avenues for her talent. Drawing on the same confidence she had exuded when she held a tennis racket for the first time, Caroline threw herself into singing, psychology, and academics. She was grateful for the forced opportunity to try new things, since she would never have voluntarily chosen to forgo a tennis season.

4. Next steps: The injury not only allowed Caroline to channel her energy into different activities but also confirmed her love for and commitment to tennis. She is looking forward to losing her cast and resuming her athletic endeavors, but she now knows that she enjoys many things, and she fully intends to incorporate her new skills and hobbies into her daily life. She will probably major in psychology because her work at her father's lab gave her some interesting ideas she wants to explore through research, and she hopes to sing with a college a cappella group.

Why this approach works:

+ It allows Caroline to discuss her devotion to tennis.
+ It showcases how well she deals with disappointments and roadblocks, and how her positive energy paid off in the end.

+ It says, in a humble, endearing way, that Caroline is naturally good at nearly everything she tries, but she doesn't just coast through life on talent; she's also extremely motivated and hard-working.

+ It raises the idea of unlimited potential, and admissions officers will be left thinking that she'll not only get a lot out of her college experience but also contribute quite a bit to her campus community through enthusiasm, participation, and creativity.

How the essay could fail:

- Caroline could focus too much on the tennis component of the essay and fail to fully illustrate her successes in other fields.

- She could spend too much time discussing the debilitating aspects of the injury rather than the optimistic attitude that helped her cope with the unexpected turn of events.

STUDENT 3: GRACE (CLUB PRESIDENT, ATHLETE)

Grace has all of her bases covered. She's currently president of the National Honor Society, and for the past three years she has served as the sole female on her school's Mathlete squad. She won a spot on the student council by promising to alleviate stress, and she is a member of three additional clubs. Despite her busy schedule, she tries to have dinner with her family every night, but she often finds herself overwhelmed with homework. Whenever she has a free moment, she brainstorms new niche interests—such as Korean traditional dance and calligraphy—to promote at her school through symposiums and guest speakers she may be able to arrange. Although her campus extracurriculars are her main focus, Grace loves animals and often volunteers at the SPCA to care for dogs and cats rescued from abusive environments. She has an impressive mind and admirable self-discipline, but there is nothing even remotely resembling an athletic bone in her five-foot-one-inch frame.

That's why, after thoughtfully reviewing her resume and cataloging her experiences to streamline the college application process, Grace decided she needed some sort of athletic endeavor to further prove how well rounded she could be. She tried out for the track team, much to the shock of her parents, who had worried even before she started writing for the school newspaper and leading freshman orientation seminars that she couldn't possibly commit to *another* activity. Her classmates, too, were shocked, and didn't know what to make of her as she strutted into the gym with a new Nike duffel bag slung over her shoulder. But the coach, an amiable history teacher in her midthirties, adhered to the "everyone's a winner" philosophy endorsed by the athletic director and immediately added Grace to the roster. She was then issued a blue-and-silver uniform, as well as a shiny warm-up windbreaker that she started wearing to and from school almost every day.

The season was relatively uneventful for Grace. She frequently had to miss practice to attend Mathlete showdowns against rival high schools, and she spent the middle third of the season recovering from an ankle sprain she'd acquired during a sprint workout. Toward the end, she finally raced the 400-meter relay in two meets, helping her team place second-to-last in the slowest heat. She was thrilled, however, to add "varsity track" to her list of accomplishments and decided it would make a great topic for one of her college essays. Her transcript would showcase her academic prowess, and her writing, she thought, would reveal an unexpected interest in sports.

What's GOOD About Grace's Thinking?

In a way, Grace has the right idea; it's never good to appear one-dimensional to a college admissions committee, especially when you think you're competing against soccer-playing violin prodigies, published authors, or former Broadway child stars. Everyone else, it seems, has lived seven or eight lives by the time they turn eighteen, and it's logical to want an edge—to be the student who can, and does, do everything.

What's BAD About Grace's Thinking?

There is, of course, a fundamental flaw in Grace's plan. It doesn't matter that she has no talent for running, because a story about a girl who goes outside her comfort zone to try something new and somehow becomes the best version of herself, albeit far from the best on the team, has a lot of potential. In fact, it's an ideal narrative formula for the second personal statement prompt about experiencing failure. Grace's problem is that she doesn't actually care about track. Admissions officers want to know what you do only if it sheds light on who you are; they want depth of character and interest, not breadth of pursuits. It would obviously be much more interesting to hear about her volunteer work—such as the story of how she came to the SPCA and compassionately rehabilitated Max, a three-legged, one-eyed dog rescued from a violent home. Those topics would have showcased the gentle, patient side of Grace's personality, giving admissions officers a better idea of how she would enhance the campus community, or even how she might interact with her freshman year roommate. Also, as a Club President student type, she needs to make it clear that she does activities for sheer enjoyment and to interact with classmates, not just to amass transcript filler.

The Essay

Let's assume Grace is determined and writes the essay anyway. Despite the fact that this isn't the strongest route for her to take, there are still ways for Grace to make the essay successful. Overall, she needs to admit that her track experience was a bit of a flop.

1. She needs to depict herself as someone who thrives on challenges. She gets involved in tons of activities because she finds it thrilling to be outside her comfort zone trying something completely different.

2. She isn't naturally athletic, so sports were something she had avoided up until that point. She decided, however, that she couldn't graduate from high school without proving to herself that she had the guts and the dedication to complete a season on a competitive sports team.

3. Her nervous excitement carried her through the first few practices, but she quickly became both mentally and physically fatigued. She pushed herself to excel, but found that even though she accomplished things she had never even thought she'd attempt, she didn't have any type of breakthrough.

4. What she learned from the experience: there are limits to her time and energy, and she realized she'd simply taken on too much. As a result of this epiphany, she pared down her commitments to be able to focus on the things that mattered most: her volunteer work, her family, and her state-championship-winning math team. She struck a balance between trying new things and pouring herself into her current activities, suddenly finding her day-to-day life even more fulfilling as a result.

5. She realized that she wasn't going to love everything she tried, but despite this, she stuck with the team through the end of the season and completed her personal goal of earning a varsity letter. It was a difficult, humbling challenge, but it was valuable because it allowed her to fall back in love with the activities already on her busy schedule.

Why this approach works:

+ It's honest.
+ It's humble.
+ It allows her to mention that she participated in a varsity sport.
+ It allows her to discuss the significance of her other activities.
+ It shows that she readily embraces challenges.
+ It shows that she has a sophisticated, reflective understanding of herself that few eighteen-year-olds possess. Most kids her age want to change the world, but few are as realistic as Grace is about how they personally can accomplish that and, more important, how they cannot.

How the essay could fail:

- If Grace tried to use the formula that consists of confronting a challenge, wanting to give up, powering through anyway, and eventually achieving great success for her efforts, it would sound trite. Any "life lesson" along the lines of, "I learned that if I tried and didn't give up, I could overcome obstacles" cannot come across as anything other than hackneyed and formulaic.

- If Grace implied that the experience of running track had a bigger impact than it actually did, it would be an obvious lie. While she did follow through on her commitment, she didn't achieve anything great, develop any new skills, or change the course of her life. There's a difference between putting a positive spin on something and rewriting history.

Since Grace wants to write an essay about running track, her impulse will be to talk about track the entire time. Because she wasn't enormously involved in the team, however, there simply isn't enough material for her essay. She needs to use the experience as a foil to discuss the other, more personally meaningful things that she does.

STUDENT 4: YOU

If you're set on writing an essay about a sports experience, make sure you ask yourself the following questions first:

1. **Are you familiar with the sport?** Remember, college essay questions, particularly those on the Common Application, are intentionally broad so that hundreds of thousands of different students can answer them. Unfortunately, many of those applicants end up submitting answers filled with what they think admissions committees want to hear. The vague nature of the questions is actually a blessing, because it's an opportunity for you to play up your strengths and write about something you know. If you just played Ultimate Frisbee for one day and can't discuss the event in vivid detail, choose a different route.

2. **Has the sport been significant to you?** This question means "Did sports help you understand something fundamental about yourself?"—not "Have you been playing sports for a long time?" You've been given a chance to write about anything that you've accomplished, encountered, or learned during your life, so make sure your sports experience is worthy of being chosen. If it's simply something you've always done rather than an activity that defines you, skip it; on the other hand, even if you've just started playing a sport, it can still make a good essay subject if it's been meaningful.

3. **Can you use the sport as a foil to discuss other aspects of your personality?** You want to present yourself as a multidimensional person, so make sure you can use the sport as a launching pad for other ideas. Can your discussion represent or include one of the following topics?

   + An achievement
   + A risk you have taken
   + An ethical dilemma
   + A person who has had a significant influence on you
   + An academic interest

4. **Does the Sports essay work with your student type?** Make sure your sports experience caters to *your* angles and imperatives. For instance, if you are an Achieve-o-Tron who needs to showcase some humility, don't choose a sports story that merely confirms your unbelievable talent.

THE COMMUNITY SERVICE ESSAY

Good for addressing these Common Application prompts: #1 (background story), #2 (experience with failure), #3 (challenging a belief), #4 (place where you feel content), and #5 (transition to adulthood).

STUDENT 1: ANDREW (AVERAGE JOE, SECRET PRODIGY)

Andrew's grades fall into the B range, and teachers often complain to his parents that he neither raises his hand to participate in class discussions nor completes his homework with any consistency. They know he shows enormous potential, because his standardized test scores are off the charts, but he remains unremarkable in the classroom. He is a nice kid, albeit extremely shy, and spends most of his free periods reading comics in the library. He isn't very involved on campus, aside from being on the roster of the junior varsity volleyball team, and he sprints to the parking lot as soon as the three o'clock bell rings.

However, he comes alive when he arrives home. He has planted a few Swiss chard plants in his small backyard vegetable garden, and he has recently finished writing the first hundred pages of his magical realism novel, inspired by the works of Gabriel Garcia Marquez. Andrew has bookshelves lining an entire wall—so full that several novels have spilled over onto the floor—and on his ceiling is a detailed spread of constellations and planets, which he drew with a glow-in-the-dark pen while balancing on a stepladder.

When the time came to complete his fifty hours of community service, a graduation requirement enforced by his school, Andrew was initially very frustrated. He certainly had nothing against volunteering, but he wanted to spend his Saturdays working on his novel instead. Finally, at the urging of his parents, he signed up for his first eight-hour shift at a local SPCA shelter, thinking that it would be a breeze to spend the day playing with animals. Although it was anything but easy, he quickly grew attached to a small beagle named Tuxedo and had fun teaching him how to play fetch. Over the next six months, Andrew ended up logging about four hundred hours at the shelter. He washed cages, walked the dogs in groups of three with the different leashes tied around his waist, and prepared individual meals for each animal. The most important part of his job was sorting through adoption applications and interviewing prospective parents for the animals, and he was proud to have placed over fifty pets in good homes. It was bittersweet when a young couple came to adopt Tuxedo, but Andrew was grateful that the dog would finally have a yard to run around in. When his senior year began, Andrew quickly zeroed in on his SPCA experience after browsing the personal statement topics on the Common Application website.

What's GOOD About Andrew's Thinking?

This is definitely the best direction for Andrew, given his personality and transcript. Unfortunately, the disparity between his grades and test scores will paint him as someone with tremendous potential impeded by a lack of motivation, and very few colleges want to take on a student who will be dead weight in an otherwise energetic and involved freshman class. However, despite what the numbers suggest, Andrew is a very intellectually curious young man who simply prefers to explore ideas on his own. Describing a selfless activity that sparked passion and required enormous commitment will refute any negative assumptions that admissions committees might otherwise make about Andrew. It will prove that he, like many students, simply needs the right incentive in order to apply himself. He can paint his SPCA experience as a transition into adulthood, when he willingly accepted new responsibilities instead of channeling his energy into solitary activities, or he can describe the shelter as the place where he feels perfectly content.

What's BAD About Andrew's Thinking?

Honestly? Nothing. His passion for the topic is sincere, and it will showcase some really admirable traits.

The Essay

Let's assume Andrew goes ahead with the essay. Andrew is in a great position, but he still needs to make sure he presents the topic in a fresh, compelling way. Here are some suggestions:

1. Start *in medias res* (in the middle of things). Andrew can use the element of surprise as he interviews the candidates who have come to adopt Tuxedo. Readers will be hooked as they struggle to guess the nature of this rigorous interview.

2. When Andrew deems the people to be worthy parents, he brings out a very excited black-and-white beagle and says his heartfelt goodbyes.

3. From this scene, it will be easy for Andrew to transition to some reflections on his experience at the SPCA shelter, beginning with the time he taught Tuxedo how to play fetch. He can be honest about how nervous and uncomfortable he felt on his first day since he had never had a pet.

4. It is important that Andrew incorporate humor as he recounts a few of his most meaningful memories. Discussing how awkward he felt as he strove to get his bearings at the shelter will exhibit refreshing modesty.

5. The funny anecdotes eventually have to expand into social commentary. Here, as the essay winds down, Andrew can examine what he learned about animal care, puppy mills, no-kill shelters, and startling statistics on euthanasia. Quiet reflections with a bit of gravity provide a great balance to the lighthearted tone of the earlier paragraphs and will allow him to show some conviction.

6. Careful: This isn't an essay about sticking with a challenge despite difficulty and disheartening facts. It's about finding a talent in an unexpected place and turning a school requirement into a significant, fulfilling commitment.

7. Andrew should resume his present-tense narration to end the essay. A new batch of beagle puppies has arrived, rescued from a box in an alley. He checks them for mites and fleas, then administers vaccinations and fills out the paperwork for their microchips. With the holiday pet drive he is planning, he hopes they will have found new, permanent homes by Christmas.

Why this approach works:

+ Readers get to see a thoughtful, tender side of Andrew's personality; his teachers and classmates may think of him as an enigma, but he develops friendships with the SPCA animals and fellow volunteers.

+ Andrew comes across as responsible and reliable, returning several times a week to care for animals that depend on him.

+ It demonstrates how seriously Andrew takes his work when he perceives merit in it. This would be an effective way to express an interest in veterinary medicine.

+ Since his extracurricular list will be rather sparse, this topic answers the admissions officers' inevitable questions about what Andrew has been doing with his spare time.

How the essay could fail:

- If Andrew spends too much time discussing how frustrated he had initially been with the prospect of community service, no subsequent discussion of personal growth can fully erase the negative first impression he will have given his readers.

- If Andrew simply analyzes what he gained instead of giving detailed accounts of his experiences, the essay will be boring to read.

STUDENT 2: KIMBERLY (UN-NATURAL, DABBLER)

Kimberly's grades fall consistently in the A– range, and since she studies incessantly to maintain her average, she is annoyed by the other students in her honors classes who can pull off perfect scores seemingly without effort. She takes great pride in having a schedule packed with APs, although she doesn't stand out in any of her courses. During conferences, her teachers note that Kimberly is organized almost to a fault, with neatly labeled binders, folders, note cards, and locker shelves, and that she takes meticulous notes whenever her teachers speak. They also tell her parents that Kimberly excels at rote memorization, but has difficulty providing independent analysis and formulating creative solutions. While her self-discipline is admirable, she neglects to pair it with imaginative inquiry and thus seldom dips below the fact-based surface of the topics she is studying. This doesn't seem to bother her, though, since her self-confidence is rooted entirely in the grades she works so hard to earn.

Kimberly is a member of the junior varsity cheerleading squad, having failed to qualify for varsity because of her fear of heights and jumps. Interestingly, her dedication to her schoolwork and her commitment to sports have an inverse relationship, as Kimberly is happy to fulfill her physical education requirement with as little effort as possible. She is also a member of the yearbook staff, a role that entails fact-checking names, pictures, and ads. Moderately popular and consistently friendly, Kimberly is neither an unknown nor a standout member of her 150-student senior class.

When it came time to fulfill her community service obligation, Kimberly was, as usual, very organized and efficient. She researched various charities in her town, contacted a nursing home about the Sunday Fun Day program it held for its residents, and signed up to volunteer the following weekend. As with her participation in cheerleading, however, Kimberly's effort at the event was perfunctory at best. She smiled as she helped eighty-nine-year-old Ruth move a piece in her checkers game, and she laughed at ninety-two-year-old Leonard's stories about growing up with seven siblings, but she was relieved to meet her friends for a movie as soon as her shift was over. Kimberly returned every Sunday afternoon for the next two months, plodding through her requirement until she hit the fifty-hour mark. Though she promised to return in the coming weeks, she quickly resumed her Sunday studying routine and never made it back to the Camden County Care Center.

As she started to draft her personal statement for her college applications, Kimberly oscillated between the topics of cheer-leading and community service. After deciding to save her sports experience for her supplements, she began writing about the lessons she'd learned by "giving up my Sundays" to help others.

What's GOOD About Kimberly's Thinking?
Unfortunately, Kimberly has very little to work with. Colleges look for depth of commitment, sincere passion, and insightful reflections, yet Kimberly's activities are merely a means to an end. This being the case, the topic of community service is neither better nor worse than any other subject she might attempt to tackle, so she might as well give it a try.

What's BAD About Kimberly's Thinking?
The obvious pitfall here is Kimberly's apathy about her volunteer experience. She will really have to work to elicit meaning from the material at her disposal, and admissions officers can usually smell this type of feigned emotion from a mile away. Moreover, the essay can easily disintegrate into irritating platitudes about the importance of service, making her writing indistinguishable from what you might find in thousands of other yawn-inducing essays.

The Essay
Let's assume Kimberly ultimately picks this topic for her essay. In the absence of another choice, it is advisable for her to proceed.

Although she's teetering on the edge of phoniness and cliché, she can still redeem herself with an extensive use of detail. Remember, specifics draw the reader in and make your subsequent analysis, however trite, more believable.

1. Kimberly should describe the grounds of the Camden County Care Center, without immediately revealing the identity of the setting. Then she should illustrate the activities under way in the residents' rec room. Here colorful anecdotes are key, and Kimberly needs to exude as much familiarity and joviality as possible. This means using names, mentioning quirky character traits (for example, Glenda is always stationed at the "connect 4" table or Liam's opening chess move is sure to involve moving his pawn to the E4 square), as well as acting as if she belongs. These types of details will create the impression that Kimberly is fully engaged in the experience.

2. Next, Kimberly should reflect on the circumstances that brought her to the care center, and this doesn't mean just complying with the school requirement. Obviously, she chose to fulfill her obligation at this specific facility, and communicating that to her readers will further highlight her commitment. Perhaps she was close to an aging neighbor when she was young, or her grandmother had recently passed away and she was using this experience as a way of paying homage to her. It certainly doesn't have to be a sob story, but since admissions officers will already be skeptical of this subject matter, it is wise to establish a feasible motive.

3. Now Kimberly can discuss her actual duties. Community service entails more than heartwarming sentiments of empathy, and being realistic about the less glitzy aspects of the job will showcase her humility, patience, and true kindness. Kimberly should make sure to maintain a tone of tenderness and devotion, recognizing that these activities served a greater purpose. Complaining will only make her look like a brat.

4. All successful essays tether their discussions and philosophizing to something tangible, normally a person. This is easy to achieve in essays about volunteering, because the human connection normally takes center stage. Kimberly should select

one individual with whom she bonded and discuss a series of interactions that shed light on her service and her personal growth.

5. Lastly, Kimberly should touch on her future with the organization: does she plan to go back? Kimberly's transcript will expose the fact that she did not pursue the activity past the fifty-hour mark, but since it is the topic of her personal statement, she needs to cultivate the impression that volunteering made a qualitative difference in her life. She shouldn't make excuses, but it wouldn't hurt to mention that although other commitments made her too busy to do community service every week, her Sundays now feel empty without Aniela's anecdotes from her childhood in Poland.

Why this approach works:

+ Even though the content struggles under the weight of insincerity, the topic offers a great opportunity for vivid, witty writing and meaningful details.

+ Focusing on the individuals she met at the nursing home will allow Kimberly to show kindness, compassion, and empathy, traits that will negate the impression admissions officers might get from her passionless transcript and tepid teacher comments. She's not just a machine that churns out decent homework assignments; Kimberly is a person with a very full heart.

How the essay could fail:

- Truly, Kimberly is in a very difficult position, and she runs the risk of appearing insincere or trite. So if Kimberly were to veer away from her detailed anecdotes and begin speaking generally about the redemptive qualities of community service, her essay would come off as preachy and fake. Community Service essays always open the door to platitudes, so she must maintain her focus on the actual experience. Admissions officers know all about the nature of community service, but they don't know about the person writing the essay—Kimberly must make sure she is selling herself, not the organization where she worked.

- Community Service essays can also seem patronizing and snobby, so Kimberly should make a point of seeming comfortable and collected. Word choice is of the utmost importance, and a single "disgusting" (even if it is in reference to helping clean up a resident who's spilled soup down her front) would derail the entire effort. Thus, while she can be candid, she must never be judgmental.

STUDENT 3: YOU

If you're set on writing an essay about community service, make sure you ask yourself the following questions first:

1. **Was the experience meaningful to you?** If you showed up to bag lunches for Meals on Wheels one day but never left the kitchen or saw the people you were helping, choose a different effort.

2. **Did you actually complete the hours voluntarily?** This means, did you simply fulfill a school graduation requirement, or did you go above and beyond what was expected of you? In a way, this is the most difficult topic to successfully execute because it's the most susceptible to cliché. Make sure you took on a leadership position, were proactive about your projects, met people who made a lasting impression on you, did it because you cared (not so you could feel self-righteous about doing charity work), and devoted a significant amount of time to the venture.

3. **Can you use it as a foil to discuss other aspects of your personality?** You want to present yourself as a multidimensional person, so make sure you can use the community service experience as a launching pad for other ideas. Can your discussion represent or include one of the following topics?

    + An achievement
    + A risk you have taken
    + An ethical dilemma
    + A person who has had a significant influence on you
    + An issue of local concern

4. **Does the Community Service essay work with your student type?** Make sure your community service experience caters to *your* angles and imperatives. This category works best for Dabblers and Average Joes who need to show a meaningful activity that helped them find their niche.

5. **Did you spend $10,000 on a trip to Africa just so you'd have fodder for your college essays?** There's nothing college admissions committees hate more than spoiled kids going through the motions of saving the world (or worse yet, thinking they've actually done it!), so make sure your essay is extremely sensitive to the various plights of others. Don't choose this topic if you're just going to preach about the pitfalls of poverty without outlining some feasible solutions you could personally put into place with the right funding or outreach programs.

Above all, a Community Service essay should be about building a better future, not ruminating on the terrible conditions that others must endure. Moreover, you shouldn't make any claims to enlightenment after a few hours of work. If your essay ends with "I now realize how lucky I am . . ." you've probably already lost your audience.

THE OUTDOOR ADVENTURE ESSAY

Good for addressing Common Application prompts #1 (background story), #2 (experience with failure), #4 (place where you feel content), and #5 (transition to adulthood).

STUDENT 1: NATHAN (SECRET PRODIGY, NATURAL)

Nathan is a diehard outdoorsman, telling anyone who will listen that he feels at peace with himself only when he's in the mountains. Unfortunately, he resides in New York City, so his opportunities to bask in expanses of unspoiled wilderness are few and far between. However, he takes advantage of every free moment to trek through the wealth of national parks and mountain trails located just an hour's drive outside the densely populated city, and he has started a Tumblr blog describing how his weekly hikes offer refuge from the incessant noise of honking cabs and wailing police sirens. He is a member of the Tri-State Hiking Society and spends his summers attending camp in International Falls, Minnesota, where he enjoys month-long canoe trips and sleeping under the stars.

Teachers often comment that Nathan absentmindedly stares out the window during class, but they still appreciate that, with his Timberland hiking boots and North Face polar fleece, he brings something different to the table. Then again, because Nathan is a Natural, his grades remain impeccable despite his nonchalance. When it comes to extracurricular activities, Nathan is a member of the Alternative Energy Club and the Recycling Society, though he doesn't hold leadership positions in either organization.

In the summer before his senior year, Nathan organized and led a backpacking trip for seven other local students who were avid followers of his blog; this trip, designed to last six weeks and cover close to four hundred miles of the Appalachian Trail, had been meticulously planned, with all the usual outdoor hazards accounted for. Unfortunately, Nathan didn't anticipate a fellow hiker's severe bee-sting allergy, and when an adverse reaction sent the sixteen-year-old into anaphylactic shock, Nathan was solely responsible for administering an EpiPen injection and running three miles to the nearest highway to flag down passersby for help. It was a terrifying episode, to say the least, and one for which Nathan, with no cell phone signal, was only somewhat prepared. Luckily, his quick thinking and composure under pressure helped to save the boy's life, but after weeks spent dealing with angry parents, he shut down his blog and took a break from outdoor excursions.

A few months later, Nathan was faced with the task of writing his college essays. For his personal statement, he wanted to write about his love of hiking, but he didn't know how to approach the subject without reliving the painful experience of the past summer's accident. After several weeks, though, he decided that he couldn't ignore this significant facet of his personality, and he reconsidered writing about the great outdoors. There is a silver lining: his story is ideal for prompt #2 about failure.

What's GOOD About Nathan's Thinking?

Since Nathan's involvement in his school extracurriculars is minimal, and his transcript will imply that he doesn't put much effort into his academic pursuits, admissions officers will definitely wonder what he actually cares about. He'll be doing himself a huge disservice if he doesn't preemptively answer that question on his own terms. The point of the personal statement is to show what makes you tick, and really, being in nature seems to be what drives and sustains Nathan, so hiking gives him an opportunity to make himself memorable. Additionally, the unexpected juxtaposition of the NYC boy being a sophisticated outdoorsman is enough to warrant a second read, because it proves that he is an individual among his urban peers. Lastly, although this probably goes without saying, he has no other choice.

What's BAD About Nathan's Thinking?

Forgive me for bringing our favorite equine, the one-trick pony, back into the discussion, but Nathan definitely runs the risk of seeming one-dimensional. Admissions officers may even wonder why he is pursuing higher education at all if he is better suited for a career in forestry or as a wilderness trip leader. Most important, Nathan's lack of foresight inadvertently put someone else's life in danger, which is an enormous red flag! The incident, if not handled carefully, could act as an application self-destruct button.

The Essay

Let's assume Nathan ultimately picks this topic for his essay. This is definitely the best decision, given his other options (read: none), but he must evince intellectual potential and multidimensionality in his discussion so colleges can understand how this passion might translate to classroom participation.

1. Rather than avoiding discomfort by omitting the anaphylactic shock incident from his essay, Nathan should actually begin with this moment. It's gripping, frightening, and very convincing as a true crisis (unlike the tragedy of losing a soccer game or failing to make the cut for Juilliard precollege after an imperfect violin audition). A boy's life actually did hang in the balance, and

Nathan had to be resourceful and calm as seven terrified hikers looked to him for a solution. That doesn't mean he should resort to melodrama, but an honest portrayal of what went through his mind as he remembered his first aid training, and the feelings of fear he denied himself during his long, desperate run to the highway, should be sufficient to establish the gravity of his essay.

2. Nathan should then backtrack, coming out of his frantic movements to consider and analyze, as he watched the ambulance pull away, the sequence of life steps that had brought him to the trail. Outlining how his love of nature first emerged in his childhood is a great way to convince readers of its legitimacy.

3. Then Nathan should explain other aspects of his treks. Enjoyment of nature can be static if he doesn't show what he gets out of it. For instance, does he use his time to philosophize? If so, he should include a concept posed by his favorite philosopher that he contemplated during a ten-mile loop in Minnewaska State Park.

4. This interest then takes on a new purpose as Nathan builds his website and cultivates a following of like-minded friends. Answering questions, sharing insights, and reaching out to peers all show how he thrives on a sense of community. This idea is more important than you may realize, since admissions officers are always thinking about the balance and dynamic on their campuses, and they want someone who is eager to contribute.

5. Now Nathan should add a few sentences about the meticulous planning and preparation that went into the ill-fated trip, showing that he was equipped and responsible, not foolhardy and overly confident, as he kicked off his first group excursion.

6. Nathan should be straightforward about the doubts he experienced following the fellow hiker's anaphylaxis. He shut down his website and spent a few weekends reading books (list the specific ones) in his room rather than venturing out. He felt a deep sense of remorse for what had happened, especially since the parents of the hiker were blaming him for the incident, despite the waiver their son had signed.

7. Nathan should end the essay by showing how he overcame these trials, eventually returning to the activities he had always loved so much. He should explain his realization that hiding did not change his circumstances, and that he was able to take his fear and transform it into positive momentum. I would actually recommend that Nathan begin conducting complimentary wilderness safety training courses at a local community center or perhaps type up a set of precautionary guidelines and distribute the information through his (newly relaunched) website. This proves that he gleaned a valuable lesson from his experience but didn't let it hold him back.

Why this approach works:

+ Tension, self-doubt, and eventual triumph: this essay has it all. From the very first line, this story should be an exciting one to read.

+ This essay is honest, and though I know I have mentioned this many times already, there is nothing more refreshing for an admissions committee, after tediously trying to dig through the layers of artifice in other applicants' essays, than to find a true person openly revealed.

+ While the story ostensibly shows Nathan's love of nature and outdoor excursions, it also demonstrates his proactive approach, his organizational skills, his ability to think on his feet, his willingness to take responsibility for his actions, and, most important, his determination to start over.

+ It's an unusual take on the typical "outdoor" essay.

How the essay could fail:

- The bee-sting allergy incident must be handled delicately because Nathan could come across as overly confident. The last thing he would want to convey would be a failure to ask about allergies beforehand—a huge oversight on his part. He definitely wants to show that he took every precaution, and that even when one is prepared, unexpected disasters can arise.

- Nathan needs to be sure that academic qualities come across, too. I mentioned earlier that admissions officers might wonder whether a liberal arts school is the best place for him, so he should prove how his interest in backpacking has given him many useful classroom skills as well. Attention to detail, for instance, is a good start. Nathan also needs to demonstrate his use of financial knowledge when budgeting and his programming skills when he set up the website.

- If Nathan ends on the negative note of the incident and the subsequent fallout, it will seem as if he is throwing himself a pity party on paper. He needs to focus on the upside and how he learned a lesson rather than lamenting how one of his hikers almost died under his watch.

- Nathan must use a mature, reflective tone, or he will risk sounding melodramatic.

STUDENT 2: COURTNEY (BUDDY, ARISTROCRAT)

Courtney is, by all counts, an "indoor" girl. Her interests include shopping, watching several *Real Housewives* spinoffs, and baking cookies. She does well in school, but that is only because it is her sole responsibility: her housekeeper does her laundry and prepares her meals, and her mother's personal assistant makes her appointments and drives her around town. She is also an only child. Her favorite class in school is French; she speaks the language fluently, thanks to her summers spent at her family's vacation home in Nice. On Saturdays she is known to sleep until noon or one, and she thinks nothing of a day spent in front of the television. On Sundays, she rides one of her three horses or attends charity polo matches. But she is not a brat; she is actually known by her classmates for being genuinely, consistently nice to everyone. She gets along well with all groups, and she will often sit down at any available seat in the cafeteria regardless of whether she knows anyone at the table. For this admirable trait she is beloved at her school rather than envied.

At the end of her sophomore year, Courtney's parents began thinking about her college prospects and decided that her transcript lacked well-roundedness and depth. So they signed her up for a three-week backpacking trip that would take her up the slopes of Mount Rainier in Washington State, and they bought her all the top-of-the-line equipment that she could possibly need. To sell her on the idea, they promised that they would schedule the family trip to France for later in the summer so she wouldn't have to miss it, but Courtney didn't put up a fight. Her easygoing personality meant that she wasn't very opinionated and could enjoy herself wherever she was.

So Courtney went on the trip, trekked through Washington, took pictures with her disposable, waterproof camera, and, as usual, made a slew of new friends. She didn't love the experience, but she tolerated it reasonably well, though she was secretly grateful to go back home to her clean bed and warm shower after a few weeks. When it came time to write her college essays, Courtney initially wanted to discuss her love of French culture, but after her college guidance officer read a first draft about beach parties and outings on yachts, he worried that this topic would depict her as exceptionally spoiled and naïve, even among her elite private school peers. Instead, he encouraged her to show how she could venture out of her element and do an unexpected activity like backpacking. Courtney cheerfully complied and began drafting an essay on her foray into the great outdoors.

What's GOOD About Courtney's Thinking?

Well, for one thing, her college guidance officer was right: if you seem as if you are pitching yourself to be the subject of a VH1 *The Fabulous Life of* . . . segment, you're in for a lot of eye rolling at your expense. Even though Courtney clearly doesn't have enough world experience to understand that her upbringing is not the norm, she should at least have a suspicion that private jets and soirees with celebrities are not the best subjects for a college essay. Admissions officers will see where she lives, where she goes to school, and the fact that she is not applying for financial aid, and they will gather a good amount about her privileged background, so discussing backpacking will be an interesting addition to her application. Remember: subverting someone's expectations about you makes you memorable and intriguing. Instead of saying that the wilderness is the place where she feels most comfortable, though, Courtney will have to concentrate on the larger picture: she is adaptable and resourceful, so she is most at ease when she is meeting new people.

What's BAD About Courtney's Thinking?

[*Deep breath ...*] Where do I begin? As admissions officers read her essay, they will pick up on several red flags. First of all, Courtney didn't choose the activity herself; it was the decision of her parents, so it doesn't show her taking the initiative to pursue an interest. Second, it lasted only three weeks, a relatively brief amount of time for an experience to dramatically reshape someone's values. Third, and perhaps most dangerous to her credibility, is the fact that Courtney never went backpacking again. If she had truly loved it, she would have signed up for a trip the following summer or gotten involved with her school's wilderness club to continue pursuing outdoor activities. The essay has a deficit that will make the topic choice unconvincing to her readers.

Although Courtney's execution of her first idea seemed shallow, her love of France isn't a terrible choice if she approaches it differently. For instance, Courtney could say how lucky she is to have had such extensive exposure to French culture. Then she could mention how she supplemented her summer immersions with French language and European history classes at her school. Did she take a French cinema elective? This would be the perfect opportunity to mention it. The essay could be held together by colorful anecdotes about conversing with strangers in an unfamiliar language, and end with reflections about aspects of the French way of life that she finds particularly appealing. Most important, Courtney's passion is real, so the essay would be fairly easy to write. Alternatively, she could talk about horseback riding, as she has consistently engaged in this activity since she was seven. However, the fact that she has kept it a pastime and not pursued competitions would need an explanation, or else she would seem unmotivated. Because she has decided to disregard these other options, though, Courtney can still make the backpacking topic work if she is clever and creative.

The Essay

Let's assume Courtney ultimately picks the backpacking topic for her essay. Since it will be obvious from the gaps in her transcript and activity chart that backpacking is not Courtney's strongest interest, the emphasis of this essay should be not on the trip itself, but rather on how she put the lessons from the experience to use once she got back home. She has to take this essay outside of nature and hiking to prove that it had long-term value she has applied elsewhere.

1. Courtney must appear involved in the trip-planning process. She must not reveal that her parents signed her up for the trip without her knowledge and sprung the idea on her with their fingers crossed. In fact, she should leave out all details that make her come across as passive.

2. I would encourage Courtney to start not from the beginning of the trip, but from the end, since this essay isn't about the struggles of scaling a mountain or battling the elements with the help of a GORE-TEX rain jacket. It's about the themes, not the context. On the last full day and night of the trip, she completes her duties with ease, demonstrating how comfortable she has become with building a fire, hanging bear bags, purifying water with iodine, minimizing her environmental impact, and efficiently packing up camp as soon as the sun is up. A narration of these activities should suffice to paint the picture; at this point, it is too early in the essay to analyze what this mastery means.

3. An interesting aspect of this wilderness trip might be the diversity of the other campers. Courtney should try to describe the scene of the final campfire and discuss some of the people she was able to meet. Focusing on differences and the quirks her new friends possessed would show her greatest gift, which is her ability to bond with anyone and put those around her at ease. Courtney should also make a point of describing, and evincing an appreciation for, her tentmate; as she is an only child, this excursion was her first exposure to sharing her sleeping space. Explaining how much fun it was to have a roommate, rather than mentioning how the cramped living

arrangements "took some getting used to," will shed light on how personable and warm Courtney is.

4. As for follow-through, this is where the story gets tricky. Courtney didn't continue this activity, so she's limited in what she can realistically say, but she can definitely put what she learned to use after she arrives home. For instance, does she start helping out more in the kitchen now that she's spent three weeks cooking on a backpacking stove? Does she take more responsibility for tidying up her personal space? Has she learned that she can live with less? Does she start spending more time outside? Does she start playing sports or getting more active now that she's proven she can literally climb a mountain? This is the time for Courtney to show how this trip affected her life in less obvious ways.

5. Now Courtney should explain her theme, which is how valuable it is to be taken out of your comfort zone through new experiences. She should list one or two other adventures she has planned for herself to show how she took the lesson to heart.

Why this approach works:

+ It's really the only way to discuss the trip and simultaneously answer the question of why she didn't pursue more outdoor activities.

+ Luckily, this approach to the topic also allows her to showcase a trait highly valued by the college admissions committees: adaptability. This doesn't mean that you should change who you are or build your identity on shifting sands, but rather, that you should acknowledge how beneficial it is to be exposed to people, ideas, and activities that challenge your preconceived notions and habits. College is all about redefining and solidifying what you believe, and if you're open to new ideas and engaging in dialogue with a diverse range of classmates, you'll be an ideal candidate for any campus community. In light of this, the fact that being "one with nature" isn't exactly Courtney's cup of tea actually works to her advantage.

How the essay could fail:

- A backpacking essay that talks about climbing mountains as a metaphor for conquering life's difficulties won't be taken seriously. Even worse is the writer who feigns a passion for the outdoors because she thinks it adds depth to her character or because it's cool.

- If Courtney is overly enthusiastic about her time in the woods or if she pretends that she discovered a significant interest, admissions officers will see right through her facade. She should not preach or draw cliché conclusions about her three weeks on a chaperoned trip, because then she will seem like a fake candidate who doesn't distinguish herself from the ten thousand others who think camping is some sort of hardship that warrants melodrama and excessive self-reflection.

- As with the Community Service essays, outdoors essays can come off as laughable if you mention how you took all your modern comforts for granted before you roughed it in a sleeping bag and made s'mores with strangers. As long as Courtney doesn't try to depict the experience as something it wasn't or make claims to having had an epiphany about herself and her relationship to the natural world, she should be fine.

STUDENT 3: YOU

If you're set on writing an essay about your own outdoor adventure, make sure to ask yourself the following questions first:

1. **Was the experience meaningful for you?** A single day of hiking doesn't make you Daniel Boone, and if you don't actually care about the environment, you will sound silly discussing the sublime beauty and importance of trees.

2. **Can you use it as a foil to discuss other aspects of your personality?** You want to present yourself as a multidimensional person, so make sure you can use the outdoor adventure experience as a launching pad for other ideas. Can your discussion represent or include one of the following topics?

- + An achievement
- + A risk you have taken
- + An ethical dilemma
- + A person who has had a significant influence on you
- + An issue of local concern

3. **Do you have something unique to say?** This is perhaps the most important thing to consider before you begin writing. Your essay needs to stand out no matter what, so make sure the outdoor experience you want to discuss is the best material at your disposal for getting that edge.

4. **Did you *actually* have an outdoor adventure?** I once had a student whose family had gone on a very expensive luxury safari in Tanzania. That trip could have provided her with a great reservoir of information and insights if she hadn't tried to turn it into an Outdoor Adventure essay. They camped every night in tents that their guides set up for them, and they slept in beds draped with silk mosquito netting. Making this out to be a challenging experience in the wilderness came across as ignorant. Camping is exactly that—camping—so don't try to turn it into an example of personal suffering.

5. **Does the Outdoor Adventure essay work with your student type?** While this category is an obvious choice for Secret Prodigies who can show off their wilderness chops, it also works for Achieve-o-Trons who may have been taken out of their element, or even Aristocrats who want to show an unexpected side of their personality.

THE INTERNATIONAL TRAVEL ESSAY

Good for addressing Common Application prompts #1 (background story), #2 (experience with failure), #3 (challenging a belief), #4 (place where you feel content), and #5 (transition to adulthood).

STUDENT 1: SACHA (SECRET PRODIGY)

Sacha's mother is a writer from Russia, and her father is a diplomat from India, so she has spent time all over the globe. Thus she associates international travel not with ritzy hotels and glamorous vacations but with everyday life and run-of-the-mill family get-togethers for various holidays. Despite her casual attitude, though, she has had opportunities to visit many of the world's most amazing locations and has had to apply for extra pages in her passport. Currently, she lives in New Jersey with her parents and her younger sister, Anya.

Sacha excels in her classes, partly because, in living and traveling all over the world, she has studied history, art, classics, and politics outside the pages of a textbook. At Sacha's current school, all clubs meet at the same time on Wednesday afternoons, so students are limited to only one extracurricular activity (besides sports). Sacha has chosen to take a computer programming course led by one of the juniors so she can dabble in Flash animation. So far, she has learned how to create animated walk cycles and is excited to possibly design her own game once her skills become more sophisticated. After school, Sacha is a nominal member of the volleyball team; she has played in only five of the eleven games. Athleticism isn't her strong suit, but she doesn't seem very concerned about her lack of progress, as her family's travels require her to frequently miss practices. Socially, Sacha struggles a bit. Her absences mean that she isn't completely engaged in her school community, and her apathy toward high school life makes her come across as standoffish. On campus, she mostly keeps to herself because she assumes no one can really understand her background or her life, and moreover, she doesn't want to make too many connections before she has to leave again. She is an outsider, but she is more mature than most of her classmates, so this is understandable. Sacha is quite nice, but she simply doesn't put in any effort with her peers.

When it came time to write her college essays, Sacha knew that she wanted to come across as a true citizen of the world, so she decided to discuss her international adventures. Her parents supported this choice, since they were also seasoned travelers who didn't tie their identities to one particular location.

What's GOOD About Sacha's Thinking?

The only constant in Sacha's upbringing has been movement (cue the irony chime), and her life has been lived without any physical boundaries. She sees time and space fluidly, as travel is a way of life for her, not a special occasion. In short, this is a great choice for showing her global mind-set (quite a hot topic in admissions committee rooms these days) as well as her dual heritage. Seeming open-minded, resourceful, and comfortable with new ideas or environments is the perfect way to present herself. If she opts to answer prompt #4, Sacha can actually say that it is not a single place, but rather the movement between places, that makes her feel most content and comfortable.

What's BAD About Sacha's Thinking?

The topic itself doesn't raise any red flags, although executing this idea in a cohesive essay will be a little tricky, because Sacha's travel experiences are too extensive to capture in 650 words. The biggest challenge she will face is isolating certain episodes and describing them in detail, or else the essay will seem like a convoluted narrative of adventures devoid of deeper meaning. She will need to aggressively limit the range of this topic so she doesn't produce a guidebook.

The Essay

Let's assume Sacha sticks to her plan and writes the essay. This is definitely a solid choice, given her background. However, Sacha will need to go through the following steps to ensure that her essay seems interconnected and organized with a central theme about her character. A good idea to develop is this: Sacha is most in her element when she is out of her element, which means she is truly comfortable meeting new people, engaging in different cultures, and expanding her beliefs.

1. As with almost all successful college essays, this one should begin with an in-the-moment narration. Sacha should pick an everyday activity, such as buying the family groceries and haggling over prices when she lived in Marrakech, Morocco, to show how relaxed she is making offers in the souk (an open-air market).

2. Next, Sacha should provide some background information on how long she lived in Morocco, how her parents' careers have necessitated frequent relocations, and how she has been in charge of caring for her younger sister while her parents are at work during the day. Sacha can explain how the most difficult question for her to answer is "Where are you from?" because she is torn: born in St. Petersburg, Russia, she moved to Vancouver, British Columbia, when she was still a toddler, then spent the rest of her life traversing national and cultural boundaries in two-year increments. The place where she lives now is northern New Jersey. The place that feels most like home is New Delhi, where all her cousins on her father's side still reside. The place where she learned how to ride a bike is Australia. The place where she discovered there was no Santa Claus was Morocco.

3. Here, Sacha can also describe parallel memories of buying groceries in Taiwan, Sydney, New Delhi, and Los Angeles, all places she has called home in her short life. This can be accomplished in a few short sentences. There is an opportunity here to incorporate humor as she contrasts the experiences. Clearly, the transitions between these places were not seamless, and she had many learning experiences as she navigated new expectations, layouts, and languages.

4. While explaining how she is a modern-day nomad, Sacha needs to reflect on what this lifestyle has given her. She should be honest about the difficulties that come with being constantly uprooted. She should also discuss the gifts it has given her: an ability to relate to anyone, a sensitivity to differences, an ability to think on her feet, an intellectual curiosity to know even more about the world, a particular closeness with her family, independence. She must also mention how living abroad contributes to her passion for academic classes and makes her even more eager to learn about the sites and history she has seen firsthand.

5. A good way to end would be a discussion of how excited she is to know that she will be spending four years surrounded by the array of diverse voices and perspectives that can be found only on a college campus. Constantly moving has made her crave this

type of community. Had she been a more outgoing person, I would have recommended that she introduce the "community" factor much earlier, but unfortunately it is hard to fake connections with classmates. Sacha can get away with merely mentioning how thrilled she is to share her experiences with others and learn from what her new classmates have to offer.

Why this approach works:

+ By starting with an everyday errand, Sacha shows how accustomed she has become to a new country in just a short period of time; she is anything but a tourist.

+ Depicting how she interacts with locals and carries out her routines is much more effective than mentioning a climb to the top of the Eiffel Tower or a swim in the Dead Sea. It also allows her to talk about how she is a product of many different ideas and influences, which few students her age have experienced, let alone processed and mastered.

+ This essay preemptively answers the question of why Sacha did not get more involved in school clubs and sports teams.

How the essay could fail:

- Sacha needs to cover a lot of ground in a single page, which may prove tricky if she isn't a skilled writer. She could potentially go overboard with her scenes, incorporating dialogue and unnecessary observations that put her over the word limit.

- She might make the mistake of placing the focus not on herself but on the places where she has lived. As pitfalls go, though, these are pretty mild threats to the effectiveness of her essay, and there's a good chance she'll be able to pull it off.

STUDENT 2: SAM (ACHIEVE-O-TRON, SECRET PRODIGY)

Sam is a genial kid who performs very well in all his honors classes, particularly BC calculus, and he excels at the viola. He is also quite gregarious and has an easy time striking up conversations with everyone he meets. Because he is an international student who has lived in the United States for only five years, he loves to travel and immerse himself in new cultures. When family finances prevent him from taking a trip, he explores different countries through their cuisine, experimenting with different recipes in his family's kitchen so he can share the experience with his parents and younger brother. He even wanders through the rows of New Haven food stands near his home in Connecticut to try Moroccan chicken *tagine* and Ethiopian *injera* rolls.

Sam takes advantage of school-sponsored trips whenever he can, which is how he came to spend his spring break in Shanghai with members of his Chinese class and travel to Belgium with his school orchestra in the summer after his junior year. In each place, when faced with language barriers, he bonded with his new acquaintances over cuisine.

Before his senior year started, Sam realized that his postcard collection, composed of one 4 by 6 print from every country he had visited, was becoming quite impressive, and he brainstormed ways to augment it on a tight budget. During an online search, he discovered the PostCrossing Project, through which people from all over the world create a network of communication by sharing tidbits of their lives, greetings, and jokes on the backs of post-cards. Now, when Sam gets home from school, he doesn't ask his mom what they will be having for dinner or flip through the latest issue of *Popular Mechanics* that is sitting on his desk; instead, he rummages through the mail to see if he has received any new postcards. Sam loves sending images from Connecticut and New York City to pen pals in Belize, Holland, and even Qatar. Rather than putting messages on the back, he fills the small rectangle of space with recipes for his favorite homemade concoctions, hoping that the other PostCrossing participants across the globe can experience his culture through cuisine.

When it came time to write his college essays, Sam was torn. He had been published in several prestigious science journals, had won countless regional and national math competitions, was in the running to be his class valedictorian, and had established a chapter of the Chinese National Honor Society on his campus. In terms of academic accolades, Sam's transcript was bursting at the seams. Each time he tried to get his ideas down on paper, though, the essay would come off sounding dry and arrogant. He wanted to produce something that would show a more colorful side of his personality, one that didn't necessarily manifest itself at school (the Secret Prodigy side). So he decided to discuss the incredible opportunities he has had to travel internationally and meet new people across the globe.

What's GOOD About Sam's Thinking?

Sam hit the nail on the head when he realized how simply listing his academic awards would sound uninspired. Achieving success in those ventures had been nearly effortless because of his intelligence, so that type of discussion doesn't allow for much of a narrative. His transcript will attest to his brains and drive, but what his application lacks is evidence of "the spark"—admissions officers want to see the settings or intellectual questions that make a student absolutely light up. This is a good choice for showcasing his initiative and curiosity. While this essay is suited for prompt #4, Sam can also attempt a creative take on #3 and challenge the belief that "home" has to be a physical place—persuasively arguing that home can be the whole world.

What's BAD About Sam's Thinking?

In terms of topic? Nothing. As with Sacha's essay, though, the difficulty lies in the execution. Sam may struggle with organizing the essay so that he can discuss his experiences both abroad and in Connecticut in a way that makes him interesting. He has a lot of material to work with, so he has to make sure he doesn't get caught up in a single anecdote.

The Essay

Let's assume Sam sticks to his plan and writes the essay. Before he writes a single word, Sam must select the cohesive narrative thread that will tie his entire essay together. Judging by the stories in his write-up, it's clear he needs to center his ideas around cuisine.

1. Sam should begin on his first night in Shanghai; he is out to dinner with his host family, and they want to treat him to an

authentic Chinese meal. He can describe the menu and the strange-looking food offerings that begin arriving at the table. This will also be a great opportunity for him to show his knowledge of the Chinese language by incorporating words such as *waiguoren* (foreigner) and mentioning the dishes that his host brother, Bingwen, suggested he try.

2. After establishing the connection between cultural exploration and food, Sam can talk about expanding his cultural fluency back at home. Because he is working on a research project at the Yale University Sterling Chemistry Lab, he can discuss getting off the M bus in New Haven and sampling offerings from the diverse food stalls.

3. As Sam savors a bite of Moroccan chicken *tagine*, he is mentally transported to Brussels, where he had gone the previous summer for his school orchestra trip. He remembers how, when negotiating the price of postcards, he had impressed the Moroccan storekeeper, Mohammed, with his attempts to incorporate the French and Arabic words from his iPhone guidebook.

4. Taking a break from studying a molecular model for his summer fuel cell research, Sam researched ways to enlarge the postcard collection he had been amassing since he was seven. He stumbled upon the PostCrossing Project and eagerly signed up. He can then provide some details about sending the recipe for his famous eggplant *parmigiana* to faraway places.

5. To wrap up the essay, Sam should discuss how, after returning from a three-day science conference in upstate New York with his chemistry research team, he had received a postcard that juxtaposed the skylines of the metropolises over China's Pearl River Delta with several steaming plates of *ha gaau* (shrimp dumpling) and *lo mai gai* (lotus leaf rice). Remembering his trip to Shanghai, he encouraged his family to try the newly opened Chinese food restaurant in Milford, Connecticut. His younger brother was horrified to learn that the tripe on the menu was actually stomach, but Sam encouraged him to have an adventure by exploring cultures other than his own.

Why this approach works:

+ The essay begins with a story about an adventure in China, where a host family is encouraging Sam to venture out of his comfort zone and try something new. It wanders through a few thematically related anecdotes about adventures Sam has had at home and describes how he seeks out opportunities to experience countries through their cuisine when he cannot afford to travel. Then it comes full circle, ending with the Chinese food that has become familiar to Sam and showing how Sam uses his daring mind-set to help others expand their horizons.

+ This essay makes Sam's open-mindedness abundantly clear.

+ It shows initiative: he capitalizes on every available opportunity to travel, and when he cannot, he finds ways to have international experiences without leaving his state.

+ Sam doesn't engage in these activities just for his own intellectual stimulation; rather, he likes to share what he has learned by cooking for his family or inviting them to try, for example, tripe.

+ Sam shows a genuine interest in other people, as evidenced by his conversation with Mohammed and his admirable attempts to communicate in an unfamiliar language.

+ Sam is able to incorporate details (using lab work as a transitional device, for instance) that confirm his commitments to his academic pursuits. This proves that although he is busy, he makes time for this genuine hobby.

How the essay could fail:

- There is a lot of specificity here, which can make an essay more believable but also can weigh it down. A few sentences here and there meant to answer the "where?" "why?" and "how?" questions are fine and actually help Sam explain why he would be in New Haven, but if he brings in so much science that it stalls the momentum of the essay, he will bore his audience.

- It is clear that Sam is a very detail-oriented, precise individual, but he has to keep the story flowing. If he devotes too many words to one story, he won't be able to cover everything in 650 words.

STUDENT 3: ANGELICA (ACHIEVE-O-TRON, NATURAL, BUDDY)

Angelica has everything: brains, beauty, great popularity, and enviable athleticism. Without even trying, she wields an enormous amount of social power. Although Angelica has recently grown interested in studying fashion blogs and updating her closet, her grades remain perfect. She takes all honors classes and effortlessly pulls off A's. She is also the MVP of her school soccer and tennis teams, achieving All-State and All-American rankings in tennis. She is her student council treasurer, the homecoming and prom queen, and the star of the debate team. In short, her life seems devoid of hardship and disappointment, providing her with a blissful bubble of happiness no one dares to pop.

Despite how it may appear, Angelica is definitely *not* Tracy Flick from Tom Perrotta's *Election*: quite the opposite, actually. She is cordial to everyone and is far too concerned with her own activities and ideas to bother with the social drama that is so prevalent in high school hallways.

In the spring of her sophomore year, Angelica had the amazing opportunity to travel to London and Paris with her family after two years of saving up. She visited the London Eye and gawked at the Crown Jewel display at the Tower of London. She strolled along the Thames, saw *Twelfth Night* in the new Globe Theater, and wandered around Harrods. Then she took the Chunnel to France, where she snapped a photo of herself in front of the Eiffel Tower to use as her new Facebook profile picture.

When it came time to write her college essays, Angelica immediately knew she wanted to discuss her trip to Europe, even though her activities and achievements provided a better reservoir of material for her to draw from. Her college adviser discouraged this approach because he thought it lacked substance, but Angelica was persistent.

What's GOOD About Angelica's Thinking?

Certainly, international travel experiences are generally interesting since they offer different lenses through which you can reevaluate your beliefs, but that doesn't mean they are inherently deep or significant. Angelica can possibly use this topic to show how she expanded her horizons and her understanding of her more limited high school world, but at the end of the day, a vacation is just a vacation. Basically, very little is "good" about this direction for her essay.

What's BAD About Angelica's Thinking?

One might argue that this trip did not challenge Angelica. It did not bring new ideas to light or show her a side of humanity she had not yet experienced. She wandered around a department store, saw a play, and posed for pictures, which are all activities she could just as easily have done in her hometown. In fact, when one considers the themes Angelica might try to discuss, the fact that she was in a foreign country is an inconsequential detail. Even so, she can try to respond to prompt #5 (transition to adulthood) and show herself becoming more independent.

The Essay

Let's assume Angelica sticks to her plan and writes the essay. She's not doing herself any favors, but here we go:

1. Angelica needs to figure out what she got out of this trip—and no, I don't mean the red phone booth figurine she picked up from a souvenir shop in London. She must figure out exactly what she wants to say about herself in this essay. A piece of advice: the theme cannot be "I learned how people around the world are not so different from me." Definitely make connections with new people, but don't take a detour into the downward spiral of generalizations.

2. Keep in mind we are grasping at straws here, but I think Angelica can describe a scene in which she got to put her school French lessons to work and experience the real-world applications of her classroom knowledge. She can also show a moment in which she had to be resourceful and independent

in a foreign environment. Perhaps she got separated from her family and had to navigate the subway system on her own. Maybe her family wanted to go shopping and Angelica instead found her way to the Louvre so she could spend time looking at a few of the paintings she had studied in her art history elective. That would prove that she was taking advantage of her vacation to incorporate intellectual elements. In general, she must show a few moments in which she explored on her own to learn about or research something.

3. The primary focus of this essay must be Angelica's time at home after returning from the trip. Did a painting she saw at the National Portrait Gallery in London inspire the topic for her senior capstone project? Did she decide to exceed her school's foreign language requirement because she understood how helpful French and Spanish fluency would be once she graduated? Angelica must put her overseas experience to work in an academic setting to prove that what was essentially a fluff trip actually meant something to her.

4. Angelica can end by reflecting on other places she wants to visit. If her career aspirations are in fashion, she can use an exploration of global trends to explain a newfound interest in sustainable textiles. She must actively seek some career value in her trip and acknowledge that, with any luck, England and France represent only the beginning of her travels.

Why this approach works:

+ It's a moderately good essay, assuming Angelica actually has detailed anecdotes and experiences to share.

+ It proves that she is forward-thinking and sees a trip not as a weeklong experience but as a gateway for her next school project or career aspirations.

How the essay could fail:

If you haven't picked up on this already, the dice are loaded against Angelica from the start. However, the objective of these chapters is to show how anyone can write about anything and manage to pull off a decent essay, so the situation isn't hopeless. That said, there are many opportunities for failure.

- There's a chance that, if this essay isn't written correctly, the admissions officers will get to the end and wonder what the point of Angelica's story was. That is to say, if she doesn't show how she used what she gained on her trip once she got back home, the essay will seem empty.
- There's a risk that Angelica will do the opposite of what she intends and accidentally come off as snobby, naïve, and shallow instead of cultured. Any talk of shopping will keep her from successfully portraying depth of character.
- If Angelica doesn't outline a moment of mental stimulation (at a museum, while speaking French, or the like), the essay won't be memorable.

STUDENT 4: YOU

If you're set on writing an International Travel essay, make sure you ask yourself the following questions first:

1. **Was the experience meaningful to you?** Please don't act as if your trip was a gift to the nation you visited. Also, don't spend your time analyzing differences between your culture and theirs; you aren't writing a research paper. Be respectful at all times, and show that you want to understand, not simply see.

2. **Can you use it as a foil to discuss other aspects of your personality?** You want to present yourself as a multidimensional person, so make sure you can use the international travel experience as a launching pad for other ideas. Can your discussion represent or include one of the following topics?

   + An achievement
   + A risk you have taken
   + An ethical dilemma
   + A person who has had a significant influence on you
   + An issue of local concern

3. **Does the International Travel essay work with your student type?** Obviously, this category can be dangerous for Aristocrats, but it can work well for Club Presidents hoping

to showcase their outgoing and intellectually curious nature, as well as Un-Naturals who want to place themselves in a context devoid of grades.

4. **Did your international travel experience give you something you could not have learned at home?** Make sure you take time to think this over, because there are few things less interesting than the tale of an eighteen-year-old who went all the way to Amsterdam just to seek out Kraft macaroni and cheese and take silly pictures with friends, all to "cultivate independence."

CHAPTER 9

WATCH IT

+ RED-FLAG TOPICS AND HOW TO TACKLE THEM +

Some students think that edgy essays get more attention in the admissions game. They're right, but not all attention is good. The topics in this section are less safe than the common essay categories discussed in the previous chapter, yet if they are carefully navigated, they can still be successful. I'm here to make sure your limb is nice and sturdy before you venture out onto it.

THE PITY ESSAY

Often used to address Common Application prompts #1 (background story), #2 (experience with failure), and #5 (transition to adulthood).

Don't write about Mom and Dad's divorce. Really, don't. The absolute worst thing you can do in a college essay is to throw yourself a pity party. I'm in no way marginalizing the legitimacy of your pain, anger, or frustration, but those are not the traits you want to showcase in this 650-word essay. Instead, show how you've processed a hardship and transformed it into positive momentum for your activities.

On that note, don't write about a close friend or family member's death simply to earn the sympathy of the admissions committee. Include it if you want (since it was no doubt a significant experience), but do not make it the focal point of the essay. *You* should be the focal point. Sob stories in which wounds still seem fresh and emotions haven't been processed will merely make your readers uncomfortable.

Here are several students who attempted to tackle difficult subjects that could have descended into self-pity and in the process wrote truly compelling essays. I hope their approaches will be helpful to you.

STUDENT 1: CASEY (NATURAL, SECRET PRODIGY)

Casey is a soft-spoken girl from Shanghai who moved to Massachusetts with her mother when she was young. Her father, a doctor of Oriental medicine, passed away when she was only six, and the scar of that experience made her an introvert. Her mother is a pharmacist who worked around the clock when Casey was young, so as an only child, Casey got used to keeping herself company. She makes stellar grades, yet her teachers are disappointed that a student so insightful and articulate in her essays never contributes to class discussions. She is an editor for her school literary magazine, a position that requires a lot of solitary work, and her role as Art Club chair means that once a year she curates a campus exhibition featuring work by her AP studio art classmates. Other than that, Casey is not very involved in school clubs, as she prefers alone time in the library. As for sports, she runs cross-country and enjoys the steady distance training that gives her time to unwind and reflect. If you asked her classmates what they thought of Casey, the majority would respond with "Casey who?" but the few students who have made it into Casey's inner circle would tell you that she is warm, thoughtful, and loyal. Overall, she is extremely smart, but she tends to keep a bit distant from her school community and engages only when it is required of her. But she wants to be more involved, and that's what matters; she just feels weighed down by the tragedy that befell her in her childhood.

When it came time to write her personal statement, she knew she wanted to pay homage to her father by acknowledging how much he—and his death—had influenced her. She also hoped that in addressing this tragedy, she could prevent admissions officers from wondering why she wasn't more involved on campus.

What's GOOD About Casey's Thinking?

The trajectory of Casey's life was offset by this loss, so it actually works perfectly with prompt #1 on the Common Application about a fundamental background or story that is central to her identity.

What's BAD About Casey's Thinking?

It may seem as if Casey is trying to make excuses for not availing herself of the resources and opportunities available at her school.

The Essay

Let's assume Casey sticks to her plan and writes the essay.

1. Instead of dropping an emotional bomb right off the bat, Casey should start with the intellectual gift her father bequeathed her: a love of the healing arts, such as homeopathic medicine. She should ease into the heartbreak with an anecdote about a certain tree or medicinal plant, then explain how she inherited this interest not so much from her father but from a quest to make sense of his death when she was very young. As she shares the tragedy, maintaining maturity and objectivity will be key.

2. Then Casey can briefly discuss keeping her father's *Natural Health Encyclopedia of Herbal Medicine* in her school locker, and how she struggled to emerge from her shell.

3. Next, a break in the clouds: for Casey's senior project, her English teacher invited all the students to meditate on the significant matters in their lives and to deliver a brief speech to the entire student body. Considering what she would say, Casey was proactive and decided to discuss her father during a chapel service. She opened up about how she had grown in the course of her high school years, seeking guidance in her father's ancient medicinal wisdom and connections with nature, while allowing other people to reach her.

   Why this approach works:

   + To really make an impact, Casey can focus on getting the style to complement the content: at the beginning, the writing will seem timid, yet the diction should grow in confidence and volume as it progresses.

- + This essay also shows how Casey uses the circumstances to become an independent young adult. She is aware that her pain has held her back, and she begins to see the positive gifts that her father's influence gave her, rather than what his early death took away.
- + Casey shows a degree of wisdom that will empower her in all her future endeavors. Most important, ending on a positive upswing shows that Casey has processed this event and is ready to throw herself into activities and classes on her college campus.

How the essay could fail:

- - Casey must take emotion out of the discussion. Sounding weepy is manipulative.
- - If Casey focuses too much on the tragedy and not how it (positively) influenced her studies, admissions officers will worry that she is not resilient.

STUDENT 2: JOSHUA (ACHIEVE-O-TRON, NATURAL, ATHLETE, BUDDY)

Joshua is the academic, athletic, and social star of his elite Manhattan public school; truly, his constant smile and kind demeanor are remarkable in such a cutthroat academic setting. A champion debater, he has won a slew of regional and national titles, and he even serves as president of his school's debate society. Additionally, he is team captain and four-year MVP of his fencing team, and when he's not training, he volunteers either at a local weekend fencing camp or with a youth debate society he founded in a low-income neighborhood. Perhaps because of his debate background, Joshua is known to spark interesting class discussions, and he is quick to offer evidence and counterarguments to coax his classmates to speak up. Unsurprisingly, his teachers adore him and nominate him for awards in virtually every subject. Joshua considers geometry the one blight on his impeccable transcript because it was his sole A–, but his "low" grade resulted from a personal matter, not an academic weakness: in the fall of Joshua's freshman year, his father died from pancreatic cancer.

Because Joshua was fourteen at the time, he was better equipped than his eight-year-old brother to cope with the tragedy, yet it still knocked the wind out of him. In grappling with the loss, Joshua made a point of maintaining his nightly routine of watching *Jeopardy*, a tradition he had once shared with his father, and he called his mom to make sure she recorded the show when a fencing tournament or debate practice ran late.

When it came time to write his college essays, Joshua's mom urged him to address fencing, as Joshua had been devoted to this sport since seventh grade, and, in addition to achieving countless personal triumphs, he had found ways to share the sport with at-risk youth through his volunteer work. Joshua's teachers, on the other hand, thought that his debate activity would be a natural focus for the personal statement, since it aligned so perfectly with Joshua's outgoing personality. Joshua did, in fact, follow his teachers' (and my) advice for his personal statement, yet he still wanted to write about his father.

He could have walked into a slew of top-tier schools, but Joshua had his sights set on Columbia, his deceased father's alma mater. At the time, Columbia had just begun accepting the Common Application and was going head-to-head with Harvard for the highest number of applications. Under the best of circumstances, Joshua's goal posed a significant challenge. Drafting his essays, he wanted to mention his father as a reason for his interest in the school, and he decided to include this information in the "Why Columbia?" short answer.

What's GOOD About Joshua's Thinking?

Since this is a supplemental essay rather than his personal statement, Joshua is taking less of a risk. Also, the word limit for this particular question is less than half that of his personal statement allotment, so chances are Joshua won't have room to get melodramatic: he will have to stay on point. Most important, his approach is honest.

What's BAD About Joshua's Thinking?

Normally, mentioning legacy status is frowned on because it implies that you expect special treatment or an edge, so Joshua will have to be straightforward when he presents this information. Also, Joshua doesn't want to give the impression that he is interested in Columbia only because his father went there; he has to drive home the point that his father may have made the introduction, but he wants to attend for his own reasons.

The Essay

Let's assume Joshua sticks to his plan and writes the essay.

1. Joshua should begin by detailing the nightly routine that he and his father had once shared: watching *Jeopardy*, keeping score on a yellow legal pad, and competing for their own personal bests. Joshua can mention how he had deemed his father the smartest man alive—behind Alex Trebek, of course—and had asked where his father had accumulated so much knowledge. "What is Columbia University?" had been his father's witty response.

2. Now, three years after losing his father, Joshua can explain how Columbia is more than just his father's school; he wants to make it his own. He can describe himself on campus, engaging in the core curriculum, discussing Plato over dinner in the John Jay Dining Hall, and using his father's wisdom as a starting point, not a goal. And here, since the word count is limited, Joshua should find a way to wrap it up.

Why this approach works:

+ What makes this idea so successful is that Joshua does not base his interest in Columbia entirely on his father's experience.

+ Joshua shows the benefits of the core curriculum in action, demonstrates an intellectual spark, and explains how honoring his father means becoming a distinguished scholar.

How the essay could fail:

- As I mentioned earlier, Joshua must seem to be mentioning his legacy status for no other reason than its role in his overall narrative. Admissions officers can sniff out an agenda from a mile away, and Joshua's Common Application will already have this information listed.

- Joshua must show why, exactly, Columbia is right for him. Often students make the mistake of saying that they have wanted to attend a school for their entire life because of family allegiances, but wearing matching college sweatshirts in your family holiday card photo does not mean you are destined for the school. Joshua must show an eagerness to engage, not just school spirit.

Unsurprisingly, real-life Joshua was accepted early decision, because his interest in Columbia was sincere.

STUDENT 3: AIDAN (CLUB PRESIDENT, BUDDY)

Aidan is an incredibly kind young man from northern New Jersey who has his heart set on making a difference in his community. He is the kind of person whose sweet smile and good intentions make you feel confident in his entire generation. He is a top student at his school but worries that he has spread himself too thin with all his academic and extracurricular commitments. In his freshman year he truly epitomized the Club President student type. That lasted only until his sophomore year, when a senior he knew from the tennis team was killed in a drunk driving accident. This incident was a catalyst for Aidan to reevaluate his priorities and drop activities that he didn't find meaningful anymore. For instance, he had enjoyed being on student council, but he decided that debating the themes for school dances was no longer a good use of his time and energy. So once his term was complete, he stepped down from his role as class representative and started a chapter of SADD (Students Against Drunk Driving) on his campus.

When it came time to write his college essays, he knew that his SADD involvement was the clear choice, as he had dropped almost everything else to educate his peers on the dangers of drunk driving. He had even done so against his parents' wishes, since they thought a single-minded commitment to SADD at the expense of his other activities would sabotage his college chances.

What's GOOD About Aidan's Thinking?

Aidan is clearly devoted to this cause, which will make his essay genuine and moving. It is also interesting that he has put his money where his mouth is and stepped up to make a difference at his school, even in the face of parental pressure, as so many teenagers have opinions on social or political ills but do nothing to alter them. Most important, this topic is ideal for prompt #5 (transition to adulthood).

What's BAD About Aidan's Thinking?

Not much—he's got conviction and he backs it up. Truly, he's in a great position, contentwise.

The Essay

Let's assume Aidan sticks to his plan and writes the essay.

1. Aidan can open with an in-the-moment description of the yearly skit he organizes, in which a smashed car is placed in the parking lot of his school and the aftermath of a drunk driving accident is reenacted for the student body. The harrowing material will be unexpected and striking, and it will set the tone for the seriousness with which Aidan pursues this cause.

2. Next, Aidan should incorporate moments of doubt, when he questions whether or not he is getting through to his classmates. He sees many of them texting or having side conversations during the presentation, and when he hears a chuckle, he is hurt that not everyone is taking the subject seriously.

3. Now Aidan can describe the circumstances that pushed him to pursue his leadership role in SADD, and how the senior's death prompted him to reevaluate his other extracurriculars. He can even describe the conversation he had with his parents when he informed them that he was dropping everything in favor of a community service initiative.

4. To end on a positive note, Aidan can explain how he is organizing another SADD event at his school, working with the local fire department and police station to bring in speakers who have had personal experience with underage drinking tragedies. He can then cite a statistic he saw in his town's newspaper at the end of his junior year—a decrease in drunk

driving fatalities—and mention how this strengthened his commitment to the work he was doing for SADD.

Why this approach works:

+ It isn't about the senior's death. Yes, Aidan knew the student and they had been teammates, but if Aidan had spent too long reflecting on the incident and made the essay about life being uncertain or short, the essay would have failed. The senior's death was not Aidan's story to tell, but the way he took that tragedy and transformed it into his own personal motivation to make a difference really left an impression.

How the essay could fail:

- Aidan must be careful to avoid sounding preachy: this is an account of his experiences and beliefs, not a lecture to his peers.

- If Aidan fills the essay with too many statistics about teen drunk driving, the essay will no longer be about him and will fail as a personal statement.

- Aidan must not seem as if he abandoned his commitments to other clubs and teams; he must make it clear he was instead choosing something more meaningful to him.

STUDENT 4: YOU

If you're set on writing a Pity essay, make sure you ask yourself the following questions first:

1. **Have you emotionally processed the tragedy, or is it still raw?** In general, death is a tricky topic to incorporate in your essays. Very few writers can address something so poignant and unsettling in 650 words, and you run the risk of either taking the emphasis off of you (you are the one applying, after all) or making light of a tragic event by rushing through your explanation.

2. **Can you use it as a foil to discuss other aspects of your personality?** Unless the tragedy inspired a constructive activity

or an optimistic mind-set, you should try to avoid it. Can your discussion represent or include one of the following topics?

+ An achievement
+ A risk you have taken
+ An ethical dilemma
+ A person who has had a significant influence on you
+ An issue of local concern

3. **Does the Pity essay work with your student type?** Be careful here. For Dabblers who never delved into any one activity, it may seem like an excuse, and Aristocrats may seem as if they're trying to create an impression of hardship. However, Club Presidents and Achieve-o-Trons can use such events to explain commitments to activities or subjects.

4. **Does this tragedy have anything to do with you?** If your elderly next-door neighbor, who used to feed your cats when your family was out of town, died when you were seven, don't discuss how this event spurred an existential crisis. Contemplating our frailty as mortal beings is never the right direction for a personal statement; stay concrete and avoid philosophizing.

THE SEXISM ESSAY

Can be used to address Common Application prompts #2 (a time when you experienced failure, or in this case, a difficulty) and #3 (challenging a belief or idea).

I normally see the subject of sexism handled very poorly, with students focusing on their anger and frustration rather than on their response to the discrimination. Often they will rant about the disparities in treatment between the sexes. While these insights are obviously valid, they take the attention off the applicant and direct it toward an issue that cannot be solved in one single-spaced page. So I ask these young women (or young men, in some cases) whether the impression they want to leave on admissions officers is one of resentment or of perseverance.

Don't complain about a flawed system; show how you proactively combated it.

The most common sexism essay I see is one in which a female student feels discriminated against on her math team or in the science lab. It is no secret that women are underrepresented in such areas, but admissions officers want to see what you were up against only if it gives context to the larger story. To illustrate this, I'll detail how a particular aspiring engineer tackled the issue and impressed not only me but also multiple Ivy League schools.

STUDENT 1: CATHERINE (DABBLER, NATURAL)

Catherine's first few years of high school seem, at least on paper, a little aimless. True to her student type, she wandered from activity to activity, trying to find her calling, but nothing seemed to click. That is, until her BC Calculus teacher, sensing her potential and wanting to even out the boy-girl balance in the advanced math courses, asked the math department head to approve her for the school's hardest class. The department head pulled her aside one afternoon to do a brief interview, and, confident in her abilities, offered her a spot for senior year. After a few hurdles such as gender stereotyping, she hit her stride, and when it came time to write her college essays, she knew she wanted to address prompt #3 (challenging a belief or idea—namely, that women can't be leaders in the math classroom).

What's GOOD About Catherine's Thinking?

She finally let her natural abilities shine—hooray! She needs to take this idea and run with it, since it's the only way to prove her potential can be unlocked in the right setting.

What's BAD About Catherine's Thinking?

She enrolled in the class at her teacher's urging instead of pursuing it on her own, but she can use that detail to express how honored and excited she felt after being given the green light. Catherine has to believe that she deserves it.

The Essay

I'll let the essay speak for itself.

I will never forget the October day in my freshman year when Mr. Cooper, my school's math department head, called me into his office. With his unkempt hair bespeaking genius-level brainwaves, the "King of Math" cut an intimidating figure. When I took a seat next to a stack of red-ink-slashed math tests, I felt my heart stop. He immediately began quizzing me on limits. At the end of the interrogation, though, he turned his eyes on me and said, "I think you are ready for the highest math class."

I was thrilled that he had selected me to join a class nicknamed "Hyper Math." In fact, I was so elated that I paid no heed to Mr. Cooper's parting words of warning: "Remember: you will be the only girl there. This may not be so easy."

The weeks that followed confirmed Mr. Cooper's omniscience. While I relished the increased rigor, a certain challenge became so onerous that I considered retreating back to regular math, if I could have borne the prospect of leaving my beloved Cartesian and polar coordinate systems behind. Each day, I tried to solve this problem, to no avail: how do I divert the hostile gaze of every boy—i.e., every student—in class? I had in no way predicted what a threat my gender would pose to my peers, especially to Mason, who seemed to deem my female presence in Hyper Math a personal affront.

Mason officially named me his archrival, a questionable honor, after I notched the school's top AMC score that year. From then on, Mason's single-minded goal was to best me and to undermine my confidence. His antagonism had a wide spectrum of outlets—from his earshot proclamations of "I don't care about my grades as long as I beat Catherine" to the bagel chips he pelted me with while our teacher drew graphs of trigonometric functions on the board.

At first, I tried to mind my own business, but I soon felt driven to stick up for myself. My concentration intensified to new heights, which seemed to have the parallel effect on Mason's focus. His efforts to one-up me, and my efforts to stand my ground, had made Hyper Math all the more hyper—so much so that, after class one day, our teacher jokingly asked both of us to give the other students a second to think before we charged ahead. On the whole, though, it was clear she was ecstatic about the Catherine-Mason effect since it kept our classmates engaged and interested.

After several months at this breakneck pace, I became aware of a motivator more potent than my desire to prove I belonged: the joy I experienced when I pushed myself. This fascination with the language of mathematics—the brutal precision with which it laid bare the universe's immutable facts—had always existed in me. No doubt it would have been jolted to its full potential sooner or later, but Mason proved an invaluable accelerator.

Now that our fierce rivalry was no longer of interest, I stopped monopolizing class conversations and instead encouraged others to speak. When I became the class go-to person for extra help, Mason was the last person I expected to seek my assistance—until the afternoon he asked if I could help him understand the Taylor series. I was shocked. Apparently, his attitude had long been a facade: Mason revealed he was struggling to pass. At first, I remembered the flying bagel chips that had stung the back of my neck. But then I noticed the broken-looking slump of his shoulders: it had taken a lot of humility for Mason to lay down his sword.

"Sure. Where should we start?" I asked. The lone girl in Hyper Math had earned the respect of a self-proclaimed rival. I wonder if even Mr. Cooper could have foreseen how rewarding this moment would be.

Why this approach works:

+ Catherine definitely paints a clear picture of the rivalry, but rather than opining about injustice, she conveys how she didn't miss a beat. She reverses her classmates' misconceptions through her intelligence and poise, and she stops herself before she gets too caught up in the I-have-something-to-prove mentality. She has a flash of indignation—she is human, after all—but she quickly works through it.

+ You want to high-five her, not console her, after reading this, and that's exactly the type of reaction you want to elicit! Sure, the unexpected friendship at the end might be a little cheesy, but it was factual, and helping (instead of besting) Mason made the essay more powerful.

How the essay could have failed:

- If Catherine's account had gotten too preachy or resentful, she would have lost her audience. Luckily, she tempers her emotions and focuses on the events.

- The essay would also have failed if Catherine had used the context to elicit pity, not show how she made her mark in a male-dominated class.

- Lastly, without a conciliatory moment at the end, Catherine may have come across as smug, and that attitude would rub readers the wrong way.

Catherine was accepted early action to her first-choice Ivy.

STUDENT 2: YOU

If you're set on writing a Sexism essay, make sure you ask yourself the following questions first:

1. **Do you intend to rant about injustice?** Save your breath: everyone is on your side, I promise. To be well received, college essays need positive energy, so make sure you can tell a motivational story about your own experiences within the larger context of sexism.

2. **Can you use it as a foil to discuss other aspects of your personality?** Again, sexism in and of itself is not enough of a topic, as it tells admissions officers about the world in general, not about you specifically. Can your discussion represent or include one of the following topics?

- An achievement
- A risk you have taken
- An ethical dilemma
- A person who has had a significant influence on you
- An issue of local concern

3. **Does the Sexism essay work with your student type?** This might be a tough topic for Club Presidents and Achieve-o-Trons, who seemingly haven't been held back, but I've found that Athletes, Average Joes, and Dabblers have an easier time discussing how they surmounted this issue.

4. **Did you really face sexism?** Don't embellish details to give your essay a bit more power; it does a disservice to those who have actually encountered it.

THE LONER ESSAY

Often used to address Common Application prompts #1 (central story) and #4 (a place where you feel content).

Many high school students like to think of themselves as the tortured romantic hero in their own hopelessly deep saga. They stay up late listening to Jimi Hendrix. They read *Wuthering Heights* and feel that Emily Brontë's brooding Heathcliff is a kindred spirit. They sit by the window and write dark poetry about how no one gets them. They keep a journal. I am familiar with this phenomenon: as a sixteen-year-old girl, I would crawl out onto my roof and work on a novel I titled *The Infinite Sadness*. Seriously. That is why I know how ridiculous the "I sit alone and think deep, existential thoughts" essay theme sounds to older readers.

A troubling trend I have seen is one of students, particularly Secret Prodigy types, using essay prompt #4 (a place where you feel at home) as a launching pad for the Loner essay. I had a student attempt a draft about locking herself in her bathroom, plopping down on the cool tile floor, and writing for hours while the world buzzed outside. Another student, who lived in Manhattan, liked to pop in her iPod earbuds and take long, contemplative walks while listening to Alanis Morissette's mid-90s albums and sorting out her thoughts. The place where she felt most at home, she reasoned, was inside her own head. "But this is ME! I want them to see who I am!" they each pled when I nixed these initial ideas.

Your college essay is not your one chance to be heard and understood, flaws and all. Admissions committees are not your psychiatrists. It is wonderful that you have such a rich interior life and that you are really digesting the ideas that come at you, but— and I cannot stress this too much—excessive navel gazing is an application self-destruct button. Think about it from an admissions officer's perspective: would you accept a student who will likely find a dark corner in the basement of the library and read Nietzsche in solitude, or a student who enlivens class discussions with questions about eternal recurrence and even starts a philosophy club on campus? Of course you want to show schools exactly who you are, but do not seek validation for your feelings through your applications. That is what diaries are for.

Of course, some introverts still lean toward the Loner essay, and I tell them it can be done, so long as they appear energetic and use this trait for something other than introspection. To show how this essay type can be tackled in a non-self-sabotaging way, I've provided two examples.

STUDENT 1: PEYTON (UN-NATURAL)

Peyton is the quintessential Un-Natural, working around the clock to keep up her GPA but never really connecting with her course material. She thinks she may want to be a doctor like her mom, an OB/GYN, but she isn't exactly invigorated by her weekend volunteer shifts at the hospital. Granted, she is only getting water and Jell-O for patients as she shadows nurses on their rounds, but she is already starting to question her premed college plan. On campus, she runs the coffee shop in the student center, meticulously organizing work schedules and arranging to have the profits donated to the charity of her classmates' choice. She also manages the swim team, keeping detailed notes for the coach and ensuring that each piece of equipment is accounted for and stored after each practice and meet, but she feels distant from the rest of the swimmers. When Peyton sat down to start working on her college essays, she considered writing about her role at the coffee shop, thinking it might be humorous that someone who doesn't drink caffeine could be so devoted to lattes and cappuccinos; however, she couldn't get any momentum going in her introduction. She considered her hospital experience as a topic, but her passion was lacking. Realizing that the only places where she felt perfectly content (prompt #4) were in the pages of her favorite novels, she decided to go a different direction and discuss a meaningful solitary activity.

What's GOOD About Peyton's Thinking?

Peyton obviously really loves to read, so she can play the sincerity card. Also, although she is involved in a few other extracurricular activities, none elicits the intellectual spark that admissions officers are seeking. Since she is an Un-Natural, Peyton needs to prove that she is more than a hyperorganized number cruncher; there is depth to her ideas, and reading makes her come to life. Perhaps the best case for pursuing this option is the fact that her other commitments are better suited for the more straightforward activity essays on certain supplements.

What's BAD About Peyton's Thinking?

The reading topic seems to come out of left field, as she doesn't really do anything related to reading—for instance, attending poetry club meetings or editing for the school literary magazine. Also, admissions officers may wonder why someone this passionate about reading isn't taking more English electives. But as long as she has at least an A in AP literature, she won't raise too many eyebrows with this approach.

The Essay

This type of essay is more common than you might think: the voracious reader who feels a kinship with literary characters. Peyton wrote an initial draft about her love of reading and how she spent all her free time in Barnes & Noble, but this first effort was generic and unconvincing.

Here is an excerpt from the original.

> The only place that I truly identify with is amongst the pages of the countless books I've read over the years. For others, their world is a field or a studio, but for me it's the various atmospheres and emotions I'm able to partake in by diving into a novel. I like to believe that I take something away from each book I read; each character I encounter allows me to see the world through a different perspective than my own, broadening my views and opinions. I'm aware of my young age and the fact that I still have years of ups and downs to get through, but I think I've always felt a strong connection with the novels I read because they allow me to gain insight into events that I have yet to encounter. My world is made up of pages, and I seek them not only for pleasure, but also as an escape. Reading allows me to distract myself from problems that seem to take over my life, by focusing on what authors have beautifully created for people like me. Ever since I was a little girl, my heart has been in all the books I've read. I plan to continue my journey through life this way by allowing books to teach me even more that I have yet to learn.

Why this version ultimately fails:

- Peyton breaks cardinal rule number one—trying to manufacture hardship where none exists—referencing the "problems" that take over her life.
- Peyton also talks about wanting an "escape" or distraction from the world, which is melodramatic.
- This version doesn't set her apart from all the other top-tier applicants who, shockingly, also like to read. The absence of details prevents readers from really engaging with the story she is telling about herself, and after marathon essay-reading sessions, admissions officers are going to feel their eyelids start to droop as they scan this bland snoozefest of an essay.

Trying to liven up this essay, we decided to portray this hobby as her trademark, adding details and using books as a way to engage with classmates and teachers. Taking a second stab at it, she wrote what follows.

Reclining on my corduroy window seat cushion, I notice that the natural light has finally started to fade. Still engrossed in the epilogue of my favorite memoir—James McBride's *Color of Water*—I flick on the Christmas lights strung from the white shutters to illuminate the redemptive wedding scene. I often return to those last pages to see dauntless Ruth finally embracing her roots, checking in with this literary matriarch as I would an old friend. As my iPod playlist shuffles from Enya to Nirvana, my headphones emit a ding. My family friend Marisa has messaged me, gushing over how much she loved *Kindred* by Octavia Butler and asking if I have any more recommendations for her. I pause my reading to reply that she would absolutely love *The Virgin Suicides*, and that I can't wait to discuss both books with her. Marisa's version of reading had once been limited to celebrity interviews in tabloids like *Star*, so last summer I made it my personal mission to show her how Sam in *The Perks of Being a Wallflower* had a more vibrant story than any young actress profiled in a magazine. Every time I receive one of her excited texts, I take great pleasure in having fostered her bookworm identity.

My friends know that if I have even five minutes free, my nose will be in a book. While my classmates can gracefully navigate the halls with their thumbs typing away on their phones, I've mastered simultaneously retrieving binders from my locker and making honey with Lily and August in *The Secret Life of Bees*. In fact, when classes began to wind down last spring, I started an informal book club to make use of our twenty-minute break each day after second period, and I love hearing how my friends are enjoying the various titles I've offered. Because I truly enjoy a broad range of genres, I'm able to personalize my suggestions. For instance, since Kyle is a history lover, I loaned him my favorite World War I story, *The Fall of Giants*, and I gave my friend Leslie *A Thousand Splendid Suns* because she's interested in women's rights abroad. My friend Emily, who likes science fiction works from the 1950s, has even shared a few books with me to broaden my perspective. I was beyond thrilled when my reputation as an avid reader—someone with over 80 new books haphazardly stacked on my desk and several hundred more on my shelf—made its way through my extended family, prompting my nine-year-old cousin to email me for recommendations after she breezed through her school reading assignments.

Despite helping me connect with my friends and family, my penchant for books occasionally comes with drawbacks since I'm more attuned to detecting biblical allusions in *East of Eden* than picking up on pop culture references. My friends find it hilarious that when they discuss celebrity events or use popular slang, I tend to stare blankly. After all, when MTV aired the VMAs last August, I was conversing with Esther in chapter 9 of Sylvia Plath's *Bell Jar*. To stay "fluent in teenager," as they joke, I at least keep up to date with the latest movies. Also, on more than one occasion, I've received a syllabus on the first day of a new English class and realized I had already read many of the books on the list. Despite these "disadvantages," what I love most about reading is the way it complements the rigidity of science, my other academic love. They both offer a very honest perspective on the world for me: through chemistry, I see that water is clear because it absorbs every wavelength of light, while James McBride's memoir, which I reread every few months, shows me that water is colorless because it is as pure as every person's soul beneath the skin. The pages of books are where I feel completely at home.

Why this essay works:

+ On the second go-round, Peyton is able to keep the focus on her love of reading. Now the books facilitate other relationships and ideas instead of acting as the static focal point.

+ The wealth of details makes Peyton more interesting and memorable and, more important, lends more credibility to her claim that reading really makes her tick.

Peyton was accepted to her top-choice California school.

STUDENT 2: JONATHAN (NATURAL, BUDDY)

The only thing Jonathan has ever had to work for, at least in school, are his friendships, which make his "Most Popular Student" designation on the senior superlatives page (as well as his "Buddy" student type) all the more astounding. A math whiz and computer programming genius, Jonathan used to keep to himself in the computer science lounge on the third floor of his school campus, solving problem sets by himself. Jonathan has suffered from eczema since early adolescence, and his self-consciousness about his skin had made him retreat into his shell, assuming others would judge him. He hated meeting new people because he thought they would be too preoccupied with looking at his skin to hear what he was saying. In fact, the first time I Skyped with him in his freshman year, he refused to turn on the video for fear that I would see what he looked like. And then he had a change of heart. Sometime in his junior fall, Jonathan decided he had to stop hiding from the world and instead confront it on his own terms. So when it came time to write his college essays, rather than focusing on his science and math competition awards or summer research projects on the Steiner ratio and mining sequential patterns, he chose to address his skin condition.

What's GOOD About Jonathan's Thinking?

When admissions officers see Jonathan's transcript, packed with math and science accolades and a checkmark next to engineering as his intended field of study, they will think they have him all figured out. That's what makes this choice interesting: readers will never see it coming, and for such an accomplished man to admit insecurity takes guts.

What's BAD About Jonathan's Thinking?

This topic is dangerous for two reasons: it could seem as if he is throwing himself a pity party, and he could come across as insecure as he attempts to make peace with his appearance.

The Essay

Still, Jonathan insisted on going in this direction. Here's how the essay turned out.

> The itching never stops. I scratch my scalp and like a spider, the itch flits to my back. I can't win. The pest constantly eludes me.
>
> I don't remember when it started. After puberty? Definitely before high school. It was minor at first, a mere inconvenience. But it worsened until it became impossible to ignore. Each doctor referred me to specialists: dermatologists, allergists, and endocrinologists. Ignoring the exorbitant fees, my parents paid out of pocket because specialists were not covered by their insurance. Impressive, unusual, rare were words I often heard from doctors. Hope swelled with each new appointment and pharmaceutical. But nothing ever works—only temporary solutions and temporary relief.
>
> Each night, I look in the mirror and see the familiar scaling and dark spots on my face. When my skin disorder was still in its nascence I thought: It will pass. As it progressed, I mused: Why me? Now, I try to affect a demeanor of nonchalance. People flinch when they first see me, and I catch the whispered comments when I walk by in the crowded hallways. The worst are the ones meant to be kind. Don't they know that I hear them say, "He must not notice because he's so easygoing"? Sometimes I lightheartedly joke back, reminding myself that no one ever died of itching.
>
> This past summer, I picked up a copy of Dylan Thomas's *Adventures in the Skin Trade* in the Strand bookstore after

I saw it on my dermatologist's desk. I confess I was initially attracted to the title, thinking it might have relevance for me. I took heart in Thomas's lighthearted views on life's tragedies. We shed skin with each new phase of life we enter, only we don't realize it until we look back and see the discarded heap. When I reflect on my own adventures in the skin trade, I know that I have developed some positive traits because of my situation. For instance, I always make an effort to be outgoing so that my skin takes a backseat. This summer, at the [specific summer program], I expected fellow participants to initially feel awkward and shy around each other. So, I arrived early on the first day of data mining class and instructed, "Find someone wearing the same color shirt as you are." Donning my favorite cobalt T-shirt, I made my way to a cluster of students also in blue, and introduced myself. As this exercise proceeded, our undergraduate professor arrived and excitedly joined in. I was amused when I learned that several students had assumed I was the teacher, but we were all grateful for the resulting class chemistry we shared during brainstorming sessions on improving computational software.

Additionally, I know that the friends I have like me for what I bring to the conversation and how I make them feel at ease. For example, last fall, I initiated informal, daily roundtable discussions in the Computer Science Department lounge, where my friends and I often do homework after school. Because I tend to bring in articles on music to help launch our dialogue, my friends have nicknamed me Jean Valjean as a reference to the Les Misérables character whose songs I know by heart. These classmates, and a few computer science teachers who frequently join in, appreciate how I even sing the equations from my problem sets as I work on them and greet people in the hall with a harmonic hello.

Each year I shed another layer of skin and move on to what is next. However, unlike Thomas, I do not want to look back. In spite of everything, I remain optimistic. Hope is, after all, the very last thing that people cling to. But, if only I could do something about the itching.

Why this approach works:

+ Instead of lamenting his skin condition, Jonathan elaborates on the positive influence it has had on his friendships. Yes, his skin issues have been tough, but they have also inspired him to be more outgoing and unapologetically himself.

+ It shows confidence and honesty, and what started as a Loner essay actually became a narrative about sociability.

How the essay could have failed:

- If Jonathan had made it seem as if he were feeling sorry for himself, he might have rubbed readers the wrong way. No one likes a "Why me?!" essay.

- If Jonathan hadn't shown what positive steps his eczema inspired him to take, admissions officers might have wondered why he was divulging this very personal information in the first place.

Jonathan was accepted early to two of the country's top engineering schools.

STUDENT 3: YOU

If you're set on writing a Loner essay, make sure you ask yourself the following questions first:

1. **Is there a social or communal element to your story?** This may seem counterintuitive, but in order to salvage a Loner essay, you cannot actually sound like a loner. Show the fascinating ideas in your mind, then come out of your head and interact with others.

2. **Can you use it as a foil to discuss other aspects of your personality?** If you're going to choose a solitary activity, make sure it allows you to discuss one or more of the following topics:

   + An achievement
   + A risk you have taken
   + An ethical dilemma
   + A person who has had a significant influence on you
   + An issue of local concern

3. **Does the Loner essay work with your student type?** If you are a Secret Prodigy, the Loner essay is right up your alley, but you should be careful, because you are already at risk of sounding too detached from your community. Likewise, Buddy student types who choose to write Loner essays miss out on an opportunity to demonstrate one of their greatest assets: their gregariousness. Club Presidents actually get the most mileage out of Loner essays because their transcripts already attest to the fact that they are outgoing, proactive, and involved.

4. **Is your topic actually interesting?** Make sure your loner activity sends the right message about you. If you like to assemble jigsaw puzzles, then the admissions committee could infer that you are meticulous and patient, but if you obsessively troll eBay for early '90s Backstreet Boys paraphernalia on nights and weekends, well, that might be a hobby you should keep under wraps.

THE "MEA CULPA" ESSAY

The "Mea Culpa" essay is not for everyone, but it does offer a solid way to answer prompts #1 (background story), #2 (failure), and #3 (challenging an idea).

Most top-tier applicants have spotless high school records. However, there are always some who have made missteps (academic or disciplinary) that stand out on their transcript like a sore thumb. Others may have faced extenuating circumstances, such as a prolonged illness, that affected their performance for an entire semester. If those situations sound familiar, the "Mea Culpa" essay is your chance to explain away the asterisks and question marks. When admissions officers wonder—and they absolutely will wonder—why there's a discernible dip in your junior spring grades or a sudden departure from the basketball team after three years on varsity, don't you want to address the confusing blips on your own terms?

If you've been suspended or expelled, you may be asked to explain the infraction in a separate, supplementary response, so don't feel you must bring it up in your personal statement. This is more of a PR opportunity to put a positive spin on something that might otherwise raise questions. Go ahead and keep the admissions committee head-scratching at bay by telling your side of the story, as long as there's a relevant story to tell.

Rules for "Mea Culpa" essays:

+ Don't get defensive. This will make the issue seem like a much bigger deal than it is. Play it cool and don't draw additional attention to it.

+ Don't sweat the small stuff. Use this type of essay only for really obvious anomalies. If you earned a detention for wearing white instead of navy blue socks to formal Wednesday chapel or you got an A– on your AP Spanish final because you forgot to bring your textbook to study on the bus to your out-of-town lacrosse game the previous afternoon, trust me, a "Mea Culpa" essay will only make you look anxious and out of touch.

+ Don't point fingers. This is not a blame game. Show maturity by taking responsibility for your actions and decisions.

+ End on a positive note—show what you learned, how you changed, what you did to make up for it, and how good you are at moving on.

To illustrate the occasions when a "Mea Culpa" essay might be appropriate, I've profiled a few students who effectively used them.

STUDENT 1: NICOLE (ARISTOCRAT, NATURAL)

A highly intelligent and capable student, Nicole spent her freshman year breezing through her honors courses. So, when arranging her sophomore year schedule, she didn't think twice about enrolling in the multitude of upper-level courses her teachers had recommended. The problem was, her school's accelerated chemistry and precalculus combination was notoriously hard, forcing even the best students into after-school tutoring sessions just to survive the course load. In addition to this daunting academic duo, Nicole had packed her schedule with APs, electives, and independent studies, choosing to forfeit her lunch period against the advice of her parents. The problem was, as a Natural, Nicole had never really learned how to apply a little elbow grease to her studies, so when she found herself floundering in the second week, she assumed the material would eventually just click.

Nicole was too stubborn to ask for help or admit defeat, so she plodded along in disbelief that she didn't just naturally "get it." Unfortunately, Nicole's sophomore fall ended up being a complete disaster, but even after sinking her GPA and dropping varsity field hockey and improv club, she still had too much pride to transfer into easier classes. She eventually pulled off a decent average in the spring, but she dropped most of her remaining extracurriculars in her junior and senior years to focus entirely on salvaging her GPA.

When it came time to write her personal statement, Nicole was set on doing a "Mea Culpa" essay because she was self-conscious about her GPA-busting sophomore fall. She knew she had the drive and academic promise to thrive at a top-tier school, but her transcript told a much different story.

What Was GOOD About Nicole's Thinking?
Nicole was a very bright girl who essentially sabotaged herself by taking on more than she could handle. Her transcript did not reflect her potential, so it was important for her to acknowledge the decisions that had hampered her high school success. Additionally, since she'd had to drop so many of her activities, Nicole had limited options. What else could she really talk about without the conversation coming back to her "mea culpa" situation?

What Was BAD About Nicole's Thinking?
She would be defining her entire high school career by a few missteps instead of focusing on the good—a risk every "Mea Culpa" essay writer takes.

The Essay
Seeing how the benefits outweighed the potential setbacks, Nicole went ahead with her "mea culpa" plans. Here's how she tackled the topic.

1. Right off the bat, Nicole called herself out for approaching her sophomore fall with an overly casual attitude about the difficulty of her schedule. She also mentioned that she was excited by the challenge of taking one of her school's most difficult courses. She ended the first paragraph with a bit of ominous foreshadowing, likening her hubris to that of Victor in Mary Shelley's *Frankenstein*, her favorite gothic novel.

2. Next, Nicole was open about how the topics in accelerated chemistry eluded her, and she provided anecdotes to illustrate, with a bit of humor, how she managed to get utterly lost in class. Interestingly, Nicole's teacher made an offhand remark about how girls usually struggle with the curriculum, making Nicole even more averse to getting help.

3. Nicole described how her confidence had dramatically waned when she received her abysmal report card that fall semester. She woefully blamed accelerated chemistry for the complete academic mess she couldn't seem to extricate herself from, and she acknowledged that she should have switched to regular chemistry. This is when she came to terms with reality and realized that there is no shame in seeking help.

4. Nicole discussed how, determined to turn over a new leaf, she met with tutors twice a week and ensured that her teachers were aware of her efforts to improve when they reviewed assignments during communal free periods. She eventually began to see results in the fourth quarter, but her improved performance couldn't completely salvage her previous scores. Although her score remains a black mark on her transcript, she mentioned that she is oddly proud of the efforts she tirelessly put forth to earn that C+.

5. Nicole ended with a bit of reflection: even as a senior, she reminisces about that frustrating period in her sophomore year with distance and increased maturity, taking away some positive lessons. Despite distractions, disappointments, and a few bad decisions along the way, she never lost faith in herself. In the process, she learned to face disappointment while acknowledging that she was not as intellectually invincible as

her freshman grades had led her to believe. She and chemistry will most certainly cross paths again, but in the future she will approach this formidable opponent with modesty and humility from the very start.

Why this approach worked:

+ It was refreshingly honest. Very few Naturals are able to admit defeat.

+ Nicole didn't sugarcoat anything, but she did try to stay positive.

+ It wasn't overblown; I've seen students try to overdo the "I messed up" theme by calling themselves "idiots." Nicole avoided unnecessarily self-deprecating words and kept her essay on an emotionally even keel.

+ She didn't entirely give up on chemistry; she stressed how interesting she found the material, but acknowledged that it required more time and energy than she had to devote to it.

+ She evinced a good attitude: make a mistake, learn from it, move on.

+ The reference to *Frankenstein* was a nice touch because it reminded readers that she was generally a great, engaged student.

How the essay could have failed:

- If Nicole had gotten emotional or melodramatic, it would have made readers uncomfortable. No one wants to read an angst-ridden essay. To repurpose a Tom Hanks life lesson from *A League of Their Own*, "There's no crying in college essays!"

- If Nicole had said "I am bad at chemistry," she would have seemed like a quitter who wouldn't be willing to sample new subjects in college.

- Nicole was an Aristocrat, so discussing how her parents offered to hire her a slew of private tutors would have made her seem helpless.

Nicole was accepted early decision to an Ivy League school she had deemed a stretch, so her "have faith in my abilities despite my past performance" tactic clearly worked.

STUDENT 2: SUZIE (ACHIEVE-O-TRON, BUDDY)

Suzie's stellar academic standing took a plunge in her junior spring when her migraines—a lifelong, albeit sporadic, condition—became an almost weekly occurrence. Interestingly, Suzie's family was not big on medication and preferred more homeopathic remedies, so it hadn't occurred to her to seek medical intervention. Also, as an Achieve-o-Tron, she was set on maintaining her academic momentum, whatever the cost. Although she was editor-in-chief of her school newspaper and a starter on the varsity volleyball team, Suzie was set on discussing her migraines for her personal statement. She was a bit self-conscious about a few B's on her transcript, but really, she thought the topic would show how she had been able to challenge her long-standing belief (prompt #3) that willpower was enough to surmount any challenge; in this situation, she had needed additional help.

What Was GOOD About Suzie's Thinking?

The humility factor definitely came into play with this topic. Many Achieve-o-Trons end up looking alike on paper, with essays that essentially say, "I took on this challenge, came up with these great ideas, contributed this that and the other, and made a huge difference for others. Hooray for me!" Not only would Suzie be avoiding that perfection trap, but she would also be candidly acknowledging her limits and bravely shaking the foundations of her family's no-medicine stance.

What Was BAD About Suzie's Thinking?

I normally tell students that "Mea Culpa" essays are necessary only when an incident is so dominant that you can't reasonably discuss anything else. That wasn't the case for Suzie—she had tons of great material to work with, particularly her position as editor-in-chief of her school newspaper. In writing this migraine-centered essay, she was at risk of drawing too much attention to this moderate, relatively brief lapse in her performance. Lastly, Suzie was a Buddy, and this essay didn't play to that social strength; it was all about a personal struggle with no communal element.

The Essay

Suzie was determined, though, so she went ahead with her "Mea Culpa" essay. Here's what happened.

1. She started off with an anecdote about having to skip her boarding school's 6 p.m. mandatory dinner because she couldn't budge. She described the pain, then illustrated how she downplayed it because of her family's position on medicine. She also explained her previous stance on the issue, believing her generation to be misdiagnosed and overprescribed, relying on pills to make up for unhealthy choices.

2. Suzie then showed how the situation worsened despite her natural remedies: when she actually needed to fall asleep after the dorm's "lights out" policy kicked in at 1 a.m., she just tossed and turned in her bed, staring at the concrete ceiling. Feeling unproductive, she would get up to work on an art project that needed fine-tuning or revisit an assignment that she had rushed through earlier that evening. Eventually, she would doze off at her desk. If not for the clatter of her thirty dorm mates rushing to get ready for 8 a.m. classes, she explained, she probably would have slept all day.

3. Next, Suzie explored why she hadn't immediately sought help. She had not wanted to share this problem with her teachers and advisers for fear that she would be sent home for treatment. Several classmates had previously taken medical leaves, and she did not want to be subjected to the same rumor mill or groundless conjecture about her condition. After all, she was keeping up her work. She was not failing any classes, nor was she close to being placed on academic probation. Then she mentioned how her parents had called her in May after they had read her year-end report. Understandably, they had assumed everything was fine with her, since they didn't have the slightest idea that Suzie suffered from migraines. Because her grades fell short of their exceedingly high

expectations, they kept repeating three words: "Just work harder." Their request didn't come with any tips on how to work more efficiently or where to turn for help, however. They thought that working more and getting less sleep would result in higher grades.

4. Suzie described the difficult and painful conversation with her parents in which she finally revealed her condition. Despite her parents' reservations, Suzie took the initiative to see a migraine specialist to discuss treatment options. She even went on medication to combat her constant fatigue and drowsiness.

5. Suzie ended her essay with an assessment of her condition. She had noticed a significant change since taking the medications: she was, thankfully, back on a normal sleep cycle, but her advisers and dorm mates were still keeping tabs on her. Her parents expressed disappointment in her decision to get a prescription for the pain, but she believed she had nothing to be ashamed of. She also discussed her new view on homeopathic healing strategies, and while she was still a firm believer in maintaining a lifestyle that facilitated the body's ability to heal itself, she knew that sometimes she must relinquish control to modern medicine. Lastly, she mentioned that her parents were coming around to her view now that they had witnessed her improvement firsthand.

Why this approach worked:

+ Suzie changed her mind about medical care, proving that she was willing to reexamine her beliefs and alter them after careful consideration. No college wants a stubbornly recalcitrant student who isn't at least open to the validity of other views.

+ Suzie came from a strict family in which parental authority was absolute, so it was interesting that she respectfully established some opinions of her own. This showed that she was a free thinker who tried to expand, but not undermine, her parents' beliefs.

+ It was detailed: readers got a glimpse into her world, even as she struggled to take part in it.

How the essay could have failed:

- If Suzie had focused too much on her pain, she would have sounded whiny.
- If Suzie hadn't included information about her background and how she had to recalibrate her opinion on medical intervention, the essay would have been boring to read. It would have lacked intellectual value and given no insight into Suzie's personality.

Suzie was accepted, regular decision, to six elite schools. (I still believe that she would not have been wait-listed at her top choice if she had included a community element in her essay.)

STUDENT 3: CONNOR (BUDDY, CLUB PRESIDENT)

Connor had once been the captain of the lacrosse and squash teams, a talented a cappella performer dubbed "the British Justin Timberlake" by his school newspaper, the president of his class, an Honor Committee representative, and the head of the peer-tutoring program. But in spring of his junior year, an error in judgment cost him a number of these positions. One of Connor's lacrosse teammates and friends had been using performance-enhancing drugs and dealing them to other school athletes, and when Connor found out, he kept his mouth shut. When his lacrosse coach grew suspicious, he confidentially approached Connor to see what he knew, but Connor still stayed silent, for fear of betraying his good friend. He was quite the Buddy student type, valuing loyalty above all. When the athletic department caught wind of the illicit activities, the students who had dealt the drugs, as well as those who had purchased and used them, were swiftly expelled. Although Connor hadn't personally taken part, he owned up to his lying and was suspended. Forced to quit the team and relinquish his roles in student government and the Honor Committee, Connor was devastated. He willingly stepped down from the peer-tutoring council, since he no longer deemed himself a role model to younger students. Although the repercussions imposed by the school administration were severe, Connor's guilt was worse, and he felt that he had derailed his entire high school career.

When it came time to apply to college, Connor decided he wanted to address prompt #5 (transition to adulthood) and show how he had learned a tough lesson in accountability.

What Was GOOD About Connor's Thinking?

A "Mea Culpa" essay was actually the ideal direction for Connor to take, given that he could show personal growth, express remorse, and simultaneously explain why his Club President status had been compromised. Admissions officers would no doubt be curious about a scandal that resulted in a suspension for such a straight shooter, so it was good for him to reveal the story in his own words. More important, his Club President student type needed to be paired with a personality-driven (rather than activity-driven) essay, so Connor had to give insight into his character anyway.

What Was BAD About Connor's Thinking?

This wasn't the most flattering impression of Connor, but to be honest, the pros outweighed the cons.

The Essay

Connor wrote his "Mea Culpa" essay as follows:

1. He started with a scene at his friend Landon's house—with Landon's name changed for privacy's sake—on the night before the lacrosse season's spring tryouts. When Connor joked that he was still out of shape from winter break, Landon offered him performance-enhancing drugs. Connor was, of course, shocked, and declined. The next day on the field, Connor watched Landon dominate the running drills with explosive speed, earning praise from their coach, and he considered how well he might have been playing if he had accepted Landon's offer. Reverie aside, he knew he had made the right decision, yet he couldn't help but notice Landon having covert conversations with several teammates in the far corner of the locker room after practice.

2. Next, Connor reflected on his decade-long friendship with Landon to reinforce why he didn't expose the drug use right away. Connor was a member of the Honor Committee, after all, so it was doubly bad for him to conceal such an egregious

infraction. Through brief but lively anecdotes, including one in which he tattled on Landon in their youth, Connor made it clear that Landon was one of his closest friends. He hoped that Landon would get caught, but he didn't want to personally turn him in.

3. Then came the confrontation with his lacrosse coach, when Connor denied all knowledge of foul play. Connor immediately knew that by lying, he was subverting the values he stood for. Expressing penitence was key here, since feeling bad only after getting punished would have made it seem as if he lacked a moral compass.

4. Connor ended his essay by mentioning the fallout, but not devoting too many words to the situation. The point was that he could have escaped punishment, but he turned himself in. Instead of being a hypocrite, he actually lived up to his goal of fostering the Honor Code within his school community, and he took a moment to reflect on how he felt about having to give up his favorite activities. He also explained his new views on being a good friend: that you sometimes have to save people from themselves, not cover for them.

Why this approach worked:

+ Connor came across as honorable.
+ The essay allowed for a lot of personal reflection, so it was not just an account of what had happened.
+ Life dishes out some harrowing lessons, so it was interesting and relatable for Connor to endure this difficult rite of passage.

How the essay could have failed:

- If Connor had sounded self-righteous about his decision to come clean, the essay would actually have been annoying. He could not allow himself to take the moral high ground.
- If Connor had harped on Landon's actions, the essay would have seemed like a witness's testimony, not a personal statement.

Connor's honesty earned him a spot at a top liberal arts college on the East Coast.

STUDENT 4: YOU

If you're set on writing a "Mea Culpa" essay, make sure you ask yourself the following questions first:

1. **Are you able to intellectually reflect on the situation?** You need to be far enough removed from your mistake that you can recognize, and articulate, its value. If you're still angry or upset, write about something more optimistic. The same goes if you didn't learn anything or you're just using this approach as a last-ditch effort to clear your name.

2. **Can you highlight positive aspects of your personality?** Admissions officers want more than a play-by-play of the event. Can you use the situation as a way to highlight your resilience, positive attitude, values, bravery, or maturity?

3. **Does the "Mea Culpa" essay work with your student type?** Luckily, these essays aren't really limited to student type, because anyone can falter over the course of four years, but they're a bit more dangerous for Dabblers and Average Joes who need to highlight strengths, not weaknesses.

4. **Is it the elephant in the room?** If not, then pick a different topic. Remember that you have only 650 words to make an amazing, unforgettable impression, so make sure the time you stole money from your roommate's wallet is the absolute best story you have to tell. In short, don't throw yourself under the bus by raising unnecessary questions; you should answer only existing ones or the ones that are sure to be asked of you!

THE "TAKING A STANCE" ESSAY

In the college admissions game, it is good to be adaptable and open-minded. Yet the Common Application prompt #3 (challenging a belief or idea) calls for having the courage of your convictions. How do you merge these seemingly contradictory traits?

I would never tell you what to believe, but please heed the following rules of thumb.

1. **Play it safe.** If you can, try to take a stance on an issue that promotes awareness and/or equality. Don't express incendiary or discriminatory views, or else admissions officers will worry that instead of promoting interesting debate on campus, you'll be a firebrand. You could also unintentionally offend the person reviewing your application.

2. **Be respectful.** Regardless of your opinions, make sure you express them in a calm and civil manner. This is not a shouting match.

3. **Understand exactly what you're saying.** This means you should do some research ahead of time and come ready with evidence. Backing up your points with details and facts, not heated emotion, makes you credible.

4. **Make it personal.** Pick an issue that has personal significance to you, and use your own experiences as a way to shed light on larger trends. Do not launch into a 650-word monologue on the need to stop human trafficking or to combat poverty if you haven't gotten involved in these causes yourself. If you want to write a "Taking a Stance" essay, it should be about your striving to make the world a better place, not about how bad the world currently is.

Here are two "Taking a Stance" essays that show how students can express firm opinions without sounding offensive or abrasive.

STUDENT 1: EDDIE (CLUB PRESIDENT)

Eddie could have written about his role as head of the campus tour guides, his experiences as a dorm prefect who mentored undergraduates, his four terms as class president, or even his duties as organizer and emcee of the annual charity fund-raising talent show. But he thought he would come across as a typical overachieving high school "hero." Moreover, he couldn't choose among his activities, since he felt equally committed to, and successful at, all of them. Interestingly, Eddie had made it his mission to cultivate awareness of the Pequots since his freshman year, when he learned of this Native American tribe's connection to his school campus. This independent effort wasn't going to show up on his transcript, so it was important to Eddie that he share it in his personal statement.

What Was GOOD About Eddie's Thinking?

For starters, he was fulfilling his student type imperative and angle by showing what really made him tick. This activism on behalf of the Pequots created a unifying theme through which he could discuss some of his other activities. Above all, using this material would show admissions officers that he wasn't just padding his resume; rather, he devoted his time and energy to a worthy cause for which there were no titles or accolades.

What Was BAD About Eddie's Thinking?

Eddie was not Native American, so although it was noble for him to take up the cause of another group, he could not even pretend to understand what the Pequots had endured. Trying to relate too much to their subjugation and struggles would have been offensive and naive.

The Essay

Still, Eddie went forward with his essay plans.

"Who was Captain John Mason?" I asked Ms. Murphy, my history teacher, when our orientation tour stopped at an upperclass girls' dorm called Mason Hall. I thought that knowing a bit of my boarding school's history would help me quickly acclimate to my new home, especially as an incoming sophomore.

"From what I understand, he was a virtuous pioneer," Ms. Murphy explained.

That evening, flipping through my student handbook, I came across a reverential blurb on Captain Mason that described him as "a wise counselor in peace." Wondering how he had earned such praise, I conducted a quick Google search that yielded articles heralding Mason as the founder of New Hampshire. Delving deeper, however, I learned that he had also orchestrated the "Mystic Massacre" in 1637 that wiped out the entire Pequot tribe. Wanting to learn about this tragic incident that had taken place only ten miles from my school's campus, I visited the library archives the following night. The librarian, Mrs. Klein, was surprised when I asked for books on the Pequots and remarked that many of the dusty books had not been checked out since the 1970s. Perusing *A Brief History of the Pequot War* when I returned to my dorm, I was appalled by how Mason had dehumanized Native Americans.

Mrs. Klein grinned when I returned to the library archives every weekend to scour antiquated texts on Native American tribes. "This one," she chirped as she slid a yellowed paperback across her desk, "hasn't been read since 1963!" As I delicately turned the pages, she cocked her head and asked, "Why you are so interested in this topic?"

"Well, I find it unsettling that these colonial injustices are glossed over in our collective memories."

After a year of researching how New England's native population was treated with particular hostility compared to tribes affected by the Indian Removal Act of 1830, I surprised Mr. Belmont and my classmates when I boldly elucidated our textbook's quarter-page overview of the Pequot War on the second day of my junior-year U.S. history class. When the period ended and Mr. Belmont approached me, I feared that I might be rebuked for taking our dialogue on a time-consuming tangent. Yet, when he smiled and said, "Rarely do I encounter a student so interested in this topic," I was relieved and immediately asked, "can we discuss how to integrate more Native American history into our syllabus?" Seeing him nod, I was excited to help my peers see American history from the perspective of those who had been unjustly subjugated.

A few weeks later, I felt confident enough to share a balanced perspective on Captain John Mason when I passed Mason Hall with the tour group I was leading. I realized that above and beyond the elements of [school name's] 300-acre campus that I loved, sharing an honest element of my school's past reminded me what I appreciate above all: how I am encouraged to question "accepted" knowledge and incomplete stories.

> While I did fear that sharing a full account of Captain Mason's history might imply that I have a less than positive opinion of [my school's] past, the tour guide coordinator reassured me that my naturally tactful and approachable demeanor showed otherwise. The visitors' nods in response to my holistic answer showed that they appreciated how I respectfully conveyed this particular historical insight. Now, each time I pass by Mason Hall, I take a reflective pause and consider how, in a small way, I have joined the scholarly effort to bring justice to the Pequots.

Why this approach worked:

+ Eddie was extremely careful to avoid implying that he understood the plight of the Pequots, or worse yet, relating their treatment to an anecdote from his own life. Instead, he discovered an issue that moved him to take action, and he did so in a respectful, research-based manner that did not throw his school under the bus.

+ This essay allows Eddie to show how thoughtful and thorough he is, and how finding answers is an exciting, rather than a perfunctory, process for him. Overall, it is nice to see a high school student wield his voice in such an effective, composed way, and several Ivy League schools thought so, too.

STUDENT 2: HANNAH (SECRET PRODIGY, DABBLER)

Hannah admitted that she felt she didn't fit in at her school. At all. That is why she dabbled in a few activities but never really dove in, and she joked that most of her classmates in her fifty-person graduating class didn't even know who she was. She was a very talented writer, though, and was frequently winning local and national poetry contests she found online. She initially considered writing a Loner essay about her love of poetry, but an incident in August before her senior year quickly changed her mind. Soft-spoken Hannah arrived at our session seething over a situation with her classmates: she had perceived an injustice, but her objections had not been well received. Her first draft had seemed angry and spiteful, and since I had been working with her for two years, I knew those adjectives were the least apt descriptions of her personality. Hannah wanted to address prompt #3 about challenging a belief or idea, so we channeled her frustration into an intellectual discussion of cultural sensitivity.

What Was GOOD About Hannah's Thinking?

Hannah seemed kind of bland on paper, even though she was an exceptional young woman, so she thought a little fervor would spice up her image. She also wanted to show that she had conviction and didn't just write poetry alone in her room. She had a point.

What Was BAD About Hannah's Thinking?

Hannah wanted to write her personal statement not on a long-term activity or interest but on a solitary incident that brought out a lot of negative emotions. If she had launched in without processing the very recent situation first, her essay would have sounded like an angst-ridden diary entry. In short, it was dangerous to tackle something that hadn't yet resolved itself, because Hannah might portray herself as someone who loses her temper and alienates her classmates.

The Essay

Still, Hannah wanted to give the essay a try. Here's how it turned out (after many, many drafts that needed to be toned down).

It is a [school name] tradition that on the first day of school, the seniors prepare posters and baked goods to welcome students and teachers back to campus. Although this greeting line was normally disorganized, our class decided to implement a unifying theme to make the day even more festive. When a classmate suggested a beach theme, featuring grass hula skirts and plastic flower leis, our Facebook group buzzed with excitement and approval. However, I responded by posting a link to a blog, written by a Native Hawaiian, about the inappropriateness of taking his culture as clichéd shorthand for exotic beach fun. When I cautioned that this move would mistakenly appropriate Hawaiian rather than beach culture, only three classmates affirmed my position with a "like." As others ignored me, chiming in with links for buying plastic ukuleles and blow-up tikis, I was disappointed that no one else seemed to have an issue with such blatant stereotyping.

Those who had initially supported me decided that wearing leis would be "a nice gesture," even though their reasons were purely aesthetic. I found it disrespectful to use cheap, plastic leis that represented a popularization of Hawaiian culture as fashionable commodities. I had no problem with honoring or celebrating Hawaiian culture, but misapplying it to our beach day seemed like exploitation.

Those who responded to my comments strongly defended the use of leis as tools of "decor and education." Many replies told me to "calm down," to not "take it personally," to "stop this weird debate," and that "nobody would care if we were politically correct or not." I told them that I cared; as an Asian, I am constantly subjected to the stereotypes of my peers, who joke I am identical to a Chinese classmate even though I am Korean and we look nothing alike. Teachers will sometimes call me the name of a different Chinese classmate. Even worse, I remember how offensive the Spanish basketball team's celebratory picture was when the players learned they had made the 2008 Beijing Olympics and pulled out the corners of their eyes for the camera. To me, there is nothing harmless about generalizations.

Unfortunately, only one person took my reservations seriously; the logical, calm discourse we shared was refreshing as I faced an onslaught of undermining sarcasm and insults from nearly everyone else. I was disappointed when the senior class president made an executive decision in favor of the leis, wrongly claiming that "cultural appropriation equals cultural appreciation." What was most disconcerting, though, was how many of my classmates were unwilling to listen.

Far from ending in a satisfactory resolution, the discussion left the basic problem unaddressed and brought other issues to light. I was disappointed to see how most of my classmates cared more about how they looked on the first day of school than about the educational mixed messages that they were sending to not only administrators but also younger students. When I entered [school name] in ninth grade, my tour guide touted the student body as a tightly knit, open-minded, and tolerant group; in fact, this belief is what had drawn me to the school. However, I noticed that when challenges to the self-image of that community are brought up—in this case, my speaking out against the popular support of leis—those glowing adjectives I had been fed on my campus tour proved inaccurate. Based on my classroom experiences, where teachers moderated thoughtful dialogue, I had expected my classmates to respectfully listen and respond even on Facebook. I still fondly look back on my years at [school name], but this experience exposed some flaws in the community's foundation; ironically, despite the negative outcome, I hope that more opportunities for debate and conflict resolution arise over the course of the year so that as a class, we can practice courteous communication skills.

Why this approach worked:

+ There is still a tinge of anger in the essay, but Hannah seems passionate about the cause, not whiny, and her complaints are backed up with facts and insights rather than pure emotion.
+ The last line really evens out the tenor and shows that she wants considerate discourse, not necessarily victory in the debate, and that approach sheds light on her character.

Hannah was accepted early decision to her first-choice liberal arts college.

STUDENT 3: YOU

If you're set on writing a "Taking a Stance" essay, make sure you ask yourself the following questions first:

1. **Was your stance meaningful?** Staging a sit-in to protest your school's removal of the frozen yogurt machine from the dining hall might have seemed like a worthy cause at the time, but

it's laughable compared to, say, working with administrators to make your campus buildings more wheelchair accessible for disabled students and visitors. Likewise, getting signatures to convince the administrators to designate a "seniors only" parking lot is not going to win you any humanitarian points. Ensure that someone who campaigns for human rights would be able to take your views and actions seriously before you make them the subject of your essay.

2. **Can you use it as a foil to discuss other aspects of your personality?** If you're going to describe your stance on an issue, make sure it allows you to discuss one or more of the following topics:

   + An achievement
   + A risk you have taken
   + An ethical dilemma
   + A person who has had a significant influence on you
   + An issue of local concern

3. **Does the "Taking a Stance" essay work with your student type?** If you are an Achieve-o-Tron or Club President, you are ignoring your impressive transcript to discuss this personal mission, so make sure your efforts say more about you than any of your other activities do. If you can, follow Eddie's lead and tie the stance to one of your extracurriculars, giving that activity added meaning. This essay type can actually be perfect for Secret Prodigies who want to show that they are filling their time with activism.

4. **Does your stance send the best message about you?** If you have to worry, even for a second, that you might sound narrow-minded or immature, go in a different direction with your essay.

CHAPTER 10

DON'T PUSH IT

+ HOW TO TAKE A MODERATE RISK +

Every year, students come to me wanting to take a risk that would make them a legend at admissions committee tables across the country. They love the idea in theory, until they start approaching their deadline and wonder if they are sabotaging themselves by being too avant-garde. Remember that thousands of "safe" essays get the top-tier stamp of approval every year, so in general, you probably shouldn't opt for the risk. Sure, it may land you a spot at a school where you'd otherwise never have a chance, but it can also backfire in a big way.

THE MODERATE RISK ESSAY

There is a subset of the risk-taking category that I call the "Moderate Risk" essay, and it offers a great alternative to the "throw it all on the table and cross your fingers that they will understand your sense of humor" essay. The following examples fall into the risk category because they don't cover traditional topics and are more about personality than accomplishments, but they still adhere to the standard essay format and provide a bit of reflection. Of course, "risk" is a subjective term. I once had a mother confront me because she thought it was inappropriate for her son to write his essay about founding a fashion club at his high school and starting a yearly student fashion show to raise money for local charities. I didn't deem this essay a risk at all, but the mother believed it was dangerous and would make her son appear "weak." A few months later, this fashion-forward student was part of the lucky 6 percent who earned regular decision acceptance to Harvard.

Without further ado, I will share seven of my favorite "Moderate Risk" essays with you so you can get some ideas. As with the earlier essays, I have changed names and personal details for privacy's sake.

STUDENT 1: KYLE (ACHIEVE-O-TRON)

Kyle made other Achieve-o-Trons look like slackers. A straight A+ student at an elite private high school, he was also president of his class and first-chair violinist of his highly selective orchestra. In his spare time he studied how to purify tea leaves, and he spent his summers at Ivy League engineering camps, programming Roomba robots to play tag. Because he had never actually dealt with academic disappointment, he had a tough time coming up with a topic that would allow for some humility. So he ignored his entire transcript and decided to write about his childhood fear of the color red.

Why This Approach Was Risky

Well, Kyle was writing about his fear of a color, so right off the bat, this wasn't looking good. If he executed the idea poorly, he could have come off sounding neurotic on paper, which would have been ironic given how collected and confident he was in person. He was at risk of calling into question the positive impression his grades and recommendation letters would make—and haven't you ever heard someone say, "If it ain't broke, don't fix it"?

Why I Still Encouraged the Risk

Kyle needed some pizzazz in his application because it was almost too perfect. He wanted admissions officers to like and remember him, not to find him impressive but bland. And there's nothing better than Achieve-o-Trons who don't take themselves too seriously, so a little humor can be very effective.

I didn't always hate red; in fact, until about eight years ago, I was actually ambivalent about the color. When I was one, my parents dressed me in a vibrant red Hanbok, traditional Korean garb embellished with gold embroidery, for my birth ceremony. According to custom, my grandparents then tossed assorted fruits into a wooden bowl and determined that I would be wise and open-minded based on the orientation of three plump, red lychees. With a naive trust in red, I later touched the fiery stovetop in my kitchen that evening; the searing burn across my palm planted the seeds of distrust. Still, though, I didn't know what to make of the vivid color, since I remained fascinated with ladybugs and always looked forward to devouring the strawberry fruit roll-ups in my school lunchbox.

It wasn't until fifth grade that my relationship with red soured. After the awkwardness of fourth-grade braces and growth spurts, I faced my first day of middle school determined to start fresh as a suave ladies' man rocking a side hair sweep and a Pokémon T-shirt. However, flashing my best smirk in the bathroom mirror once I'd finished posing for my yearbook photos, I realized in horror that a flake of red kimchi had embedded itself between my front teeth and foiled my facade of coolness. A few weeks later, when Michelle, a girl from my social studies class, returned what I would later refer to as my "Red Rose of Rejection," my abhorrence of red was solidified. I quickly swore off pizza, with its menacing tomato sauce, and cans plastered with Coca-Cola's iconic red banner. I also began seeking out negative associations with which to confirm my prejudice: mosquito bites, scraped knees, scream-inducing sequences from horror films. For the next four years, I made a conscious effort to boycott all things red, even the scrumptious red velvet cupcakes my mom baked for my birthday.

And then, capriciously, my relationship with scarlet turned. One early morning in eighth grade, I was thirteen hours into a grueling fifteen-hour flight home from Korea. As I flipped through the latest issue of *Popular Science*, I lifted the window shade and saw the warm, ruby prelude to the sunrise bleeding up the horizon. When we landed, I noted the red and blue swirl of the Korean flag painted on the tail of the aircraft, and knew that, at least out of respect for my heritage, I had to make amends with my sworn enemy.

I felt like the bigger man when I buried the hatchet and welcomed a new, burgundy piano into my family's home last fall. Even though a red "B" represents the rivals to my pinstripe blue Yankees, and seeing red horizontal stripes reminds me of how Manchester United trumped my favorite team, Chelsea FC, in the Champions' League final three years ago, I could only stay angry at pizza for so long. These days, I embrace Santa Claus, have no qualms about scarfing down spaghetti marinara, and always strive to fulfill the prophecy of the lychees.

Why this approach worked:

+ In a few short paragraphs, Kyle is able to show us how he grapples with a childhood phobia and makes an effort to move past it.
+ The metaphor at play here is also extremely powerful: Kyle is discussing society's unfounded prejudices, as well as his understanding that they are mental constructs we can easily overcome with the right perspective and will power.

Kyle was accepted early action to his first-choice Ivy, indicating that "neuroses" risks can work so long as you make them endearing.

STUDENT 2: EVELYN (DABBLER)

Evelyn absolutely dreaded initial meetings with strangers, before she could forge a connection and establish herself as smart and personable; however, once she began talking, it was clear her thoughts had an almost poetic quality. Unfortunately, though, she had trouble really finding her niche in high school. A lifelong glasses wearer, she found contacts too scratchy when she was on the basketball court. Her volleyball career fizzled out for a similar reason, when the opposing team's spike smashed right into her shoulder as she was adjusting her uncomfortable sports goggles. Soon she gave up on sports. Evelyn enjoyed doing layout for her campus newspaper, but the small staff numbers meant she was expected to interview classmates and teachers for articles, a challenge her shy side didn't exactly relish. As she filled out her essay questionnaire, she noticed that she had a smattering of seemingly unrelated experiences she wanted to discuss, but none was strong enough to stand on its own. So she decided to tackle all of them, with the color yellow, the only unifying factor, driving and sustaining the essay.

Why This Approach Was Risky
Evelyn was a Dabbler, which meant she really needed to "show undaunted dedication to a single endeavor" so she wouldn't "appear aimless." It's always a risk to write something that merely confirms your student type without obviating the concerns or questions associated with it. Jumping from experience to experience with only a color acting as the tenuous narrative thread could have made make Evelyn appear even more flighty and unfocused.

Why I Still Encouraged the Risk
Meeting with Evelyn, I soon noticed that the way she viewed and digested the world was uniquely and beautifully artistic. However, while she did have AP studio art on her transcript, it did not really stand out amid a long list of one-year commitments to clubs and activities. I wanted admissions officers to see the unique way her mind worked, as if she were actually painting a story for them. Given Evelyn's talents and background in art, I thought she could pull off yellow as a transitional device.

> Yellow is the morning mist that gathers on my window in the quiet moments before my alarm sounds. It is the pavement of my elementary school walkway and the haze that melts into the sky right before dusk. Yellow was my favorite crayon, the one that my brother snapped into pieces when I was a three-year-

old in diapers. It was the color of the sunflowers in my mom's garden that I often attempted to draw, the hue of the cornbread at our Thanksgiving dinners, and the reflection of the afternoon sun bouncing off my best friend's hair. Yellow is quietly beautiful, charming and elegant, highlighting the contours of the world. Perhaps this is why I have always loved it.

When I was in first grade, a man set up a folding table outside the entrance to my school and began selling chicks out of a cramped, flimsy cardboard box. I remember the fluffy yellow face that looked up at me, and although the small bird was visibly sick, I immediately handed over fifty cents to take it home with me. I had hoped its youthful yellow would one day darken into a radiant red, so I showered the chick with attention, kept it well fed, and dutifully cleaned the golden straw of its pen. My commitment and devotion were partly successful, as the chick became active and vocal, continuously chirping throughout the day. Sadly, though, it succumbed to its illness within a month, and I buried it in my backyard beneath a homemade wreath of butter-colored daffodils.

Even now, before I paint, I first mix the delicate yellows of my watercolors to lay the foundation for weightier shapes. In the background, yellow animates my artwork, adding depth and softness. Applying the initial touches, I immerse my brush in a puddle of mustard and splash it onto the pristine white. In oil paintings, I commonly add slight tinges of yellow to emphasize contrast, dabbing it onto a shirt peeking out from under a black suit, or onto a curtain behind a woman in a bright, patterned dress. My accents became even more daring after seeing Peter Ngugi's works up close and realizing that this artist, whom I'd always admired, illuminated the edges of his figures with bright yellows. Influenced by his color palette, I was thrilled to smudge banana all across the canvas instead of simply relegating lemon droplets to the details.

Yellow also punctuates my experiences with food. Walking down a crowded street behind the Wangfujing Plaza in Beijing, I was greeted by wafts of tofu's acrid, yet oddly appetizing odor. It was a scent that would make the Travel Channel's

Andrew Zimmern ravenous to sample the peculiar delicacies I saw before me. I found myself staring into the black eyes of a yellow scorpion that was writhing in pain on a grill. My gag reflexes were triggered as my classmates challenged me to bite into its crunchy exoskeleton. When I held my breath and dug my teeth into its crispy citrine tail, however, I tasted a surprisingly scrumptious flavor that was a confluence of sweet, salty, and bitter. The scorpion's peculiar yellow shell had inspired me to expel my fears and greet my curiosities.

Canary, amber, vanilla, and maize have woven themselves into each of my experiences. Like the thick tip of a highlighter, they have accented and enhanced my life, drawing attention to the sensory details hiding in the margins of my daily routines. Trapped between cool blues and purples and the strong, roaring reds, I remain composed in the face of hindrances as I pursue my passions for art and adventure. My emotions, temperament, and demeanor are all captured by these rays of sunlight.

Why this approach worked:

+ Interestingly, the color yellow allows Evelyn to show how she has a consistent demeanor that possesses different shades: sweet and buttery yellow, playful and zingy lemon, bright pops of fun-loving canary. She has a softer side that cares for others and willingly assumes responsibility, an adventurous side that thrives on new experiences, and an experimental side that uses yellow to brighten shapes that might otherwise fade into the background. Yes, the last line is a little cheesy, but by that point in the essay, readers have fallen in love with this sunny student and aren't going to lose sight of her endearing characteristics over one predictable sentence with a passive construction.

+ It is incredibly detailed, giving readers a very thorough and vivid glimpse into Evelyn's world.

Evelyn got in, regular admission, to nine top-tier schools.

STUDENT 3: JACK (NATURAL)

Jack, like any Natural student type, seemed to breeze through classes, sports, and orchestra with minimal effort. He wasn't as driven as his Achieve-o-Tron peers, and his nonchalance occasionally irked his classmates and teachers, but he was still admired for his intelligence. When it came time to write his college essays, Jack wasn't interested in constructing a facade of perfection, as he thought it would make him sound fake. Instead, he wanted to focus on Facebook, or rather, his lack of a social media presence.

Why This Approach Was Risky

If you ask your college guidance counselors whether an essay about Facebook is a good decision, you will most likely get a stern headshake and an exasperated "no." I call this the "holier than thou" essay, which can fail miserably if Jack passes judgment on Facebook or acts as if he is superior because he doesn't partake in wall postings (remember, the admissions officers probably have social media accounts of their own).

Why I Still Encouraged the Risk

It may sound superficial in theory, but Facebook is the perfect way for Jack to introduce himself to the admissions committee. The fact that he has forgone social networking sites makes him an interesting anomaly. Honestly, how many teenagers do you actually know who don't have Facebook, Instagram, Twitter, or Tumblr accounts?

I have the distinction of being the subject of a Facebook group. Unlike "Manchester United," "Math Enthusiasts," or "Music IB Higher," my group is titled, "If 500 people join this group, Jack Hudson has to make a Facebook profile." My brother told me that as of today, 765 people have eagerly joined.

My parents, who have Facebook profiles of their own, have begged me to get on board with this social-networking craze. They get frustrated when my twin brother becomes my social secretary, dominating our dinner conversations with detailed, breaking news he could only have learned from the "status updates" and "foursquare check-ins" on his "newsfeed." My parents also believe that beyond its social value, Facebook can serve an academic purpose as well. For example, before our math final, many of my classmates still struggled to solve $\ln(t + 1)$. Since no one could figure out the solution, someone decided to post my phone number online. At 1 a.m., I started to get calls from countless panicked classmates, which frustrated my tired parents. Explaining the same answer fifteen times made me wonder whether, if I had a Facebook account, I would have actually gotten some sleep that night. After all, I could have just uploaded a photo of my proof—where one uses the integration by parts method first, followed by the substitution method—onto my "wall."

Sleep deprivation aside, the biggest disadvantage of not having Facebook is losing contact with friends I make outside of school. As a [school name] survivor, a term we apply to students who don't simply transfer to our campus for a year before going abroad with their diplomatic parents, I've gotten to know virtually everyone. But, for the friends whom I meet at summer music programs, Facebook is indispensable for keeping in touch. For example, I tried to call Justin, a fellow clarinetist who lived in Chicago, to discuss how [name], the principal clarinetist of the [city] Orchestra, had just moved to the [city] Philharmonic. I was surprised to learn that Justin was actually in New York at the moment for a three-week summer program, and that my absence from Facebook meant I hadn't gotten the news in advance. Apparently, he did not think of making the effort to look up my number and call me when he arrived. Because my name wasn't a fixture on his newsfeed, I had apparently lost relevance.

Despite these disappointing realizations, I still feel that without Facebook, I am able to practice social networking in its purest form. When I engage with friends, I intently listen to their ideas and stories, and I hope they do the same when I'm recapitulating how Manchester United annihilated Arsenal in the English Premier League. There's certainly nothing wrong with cultivating acquaintances and touching base online, and I realize that I am in the minority here, but I still prefer discussing a particular news article with a friend instead of simply clicking "like" beneath his status update.

Even so, I may eventually have to succumb to the pressure of my friends and family and create a Facebook profile. It's becoming impossible to make plans, even for something as simple and informal as seeing a movie, using just my cell phone. Moreover, when I leave summer camp, I loathe the bewildered looks I get and the long explanations I must provide to requests of "friend me!" and "don't forget to tag me in your pictures!" Perhaps when the Facebook group founded in my honor reaches 1,000 members, or when the quick 1 a.m. math answers turn into lengthy 3 a.m. chemistry lab report consultations, I'll embrace the online dialogue that's been under way without me. Or maybe I'll hold out and see what happens when my thoughts and comments aren't limited to text boxes and thumbs-up icons.

Why this approach worked:

+ Jack acknowledges how he feels left out and how communication relies heavily on online forums. He also understands that Facebook is a powerful tool for connecting people across the globe. But he is believably busy and is living his life in the real world, away from his computer screen and without needless distractions.

+ He comes across as unassuming and different, which is a refreshing change of pace. Also, you should note that he never resorts to bragging, which immensely increases his likeability.

Jack was accepted, early action, to his first-choice Ivy.

STUDENT 4: STEVE (ACHIEVE-O-TRON)

Steve was a math and science prodigy who won recognition in national high school engineering competitions, so on paper he seemed like a nose-to-the-grindstone type of applicant. Unsurprisingly, his grades and test scores were impeccable, and his extracurriculars went beyond mere club membership; he engaged in research projects with college professors.

The problem was, the fall of his senior year, he wanted to apply to some of the country's top engineering and technology schools, so his transcript would have looked identical to thirty thousand others. As we talked, I asked whether he had any talents or hobbies that wouldn't manifest themselves in his application, and his face lit up: he had "freakishly sensitive" taste buds. One of his supplements had a 350-word "Is there anything else you want us to know about you?" prompt, and we decided to share his culinary know-how.

Why This Approach Was Risky
I call this a "left-field" risk because the content seems rather random. A lot of students like to drop arbitrary facts about themselves for shock value, which can give admissions officers a disjointed impression just as they are on the verge of figuring the applicant out.

Why I Still Encouraged the Risk
I thought this hidden talent would give his readers an idea of the social contributions he would make to the campus atmosphere. Sometimes academic excellence isn't enough to sell you, and Steve understood that he had to show something more if he wanted to stand out in the applicant pool. Above all, I thought we could connect this skill to his interest in chemistry.

> Blindfolded, I am suddenly greeted by the taste of a juicy burger in my mouth. I take a bite, and let my taste buds begin the work. Then I am offered another burger. Most people would say that they all taste the same, but to me, the differences are easy to assess. I announce, "The first one is definitely McDonald's Big Mac. The second one is a Burger King Whopper." The room erupts in cheers as I remove my blindfold and confirm what I have identified. On Wednesday

nights, my roommate likes to subject me to a blind taste test, and these experiments have become humorous study breaks for the entire dorm. I have had this peculiar talent for as long as I can remember. My parents were initially embarrassed when I, as a ten-year-old, pointed out to waiters that the cooks had used rice vinegar, instead of cider, to marinate the bulgogi. Later, however, my mom began to appreciate my highly sensitive taste buds and sense of smell when she asked me to decipher ingredients in restaurant dishes so she could try to re-create them. She took notes as I confirmed hints of persimmon as the sweetening agent in our local Italian cafe's signature seafood lasagna. My classmates also appreciate how I can, based on the aromas wafting across the quad, guess our school's lunchtime offerings and help them decide whether to eat off-campus before they've trekked all the way to the cafeteria. Distinguishing Coke from Pepsi and Dr. Pepper is for beginners; I have mastered the art of determining whether Sweet'N Low or Splenda has been used in my coffee, or even if cookies have chips that are 65 percent or 72 percent cocoa. Being a chemistry enthusiast, I can't help but notice that molecular components determine the characteristics of anything that has a chemical makeup, and that certainly includes the secret recipes of my favorite treats.

Why this approach worked:

+ Steve brings in a much-needed social component to make his skill relevant; otherwise, admissions officers probably wouldn't care whether he could detect the sweetening agents in their dining hall's pesto tortellini.
+ It is wholly unexpected, but there is a chemistry tie-in at the end to keep the topic relevant to Steve's academic strengths.

The following year, Steve joined the chemical engineering department at a world-class research university.

STUDENT 5: JEREMY (AVERAGE JOE, BUDDY)

Jeremy's wide smile lit up the room when he entered. Virtually every single one of his classmates considered him a friend, and that was no small feat at his sprawling public school. As he filled out his questionnaire, though, Jeremy's confidence waned, and he admitted that another tutor had urged him to center his personal statement around his learning disabilities. Jeremy had been uncomfortable with this direction because he worried that devoting his 650 words to ADD and dyslexia would be like saying "my disabilities define me." He wanted his personal statement to be a bit more vibrant and less defensive. Brainstorming ways to begin, he popped open a jar of olives, his favorite snack. Since Jeremy couldn't seem to find the words to describe himself, he asked if he could instead describe the olives and make them the focal point of the essay.

Why This Approach Was Risky

Jeremy set out to write a piece that, at least in the first few sentences, could easily have been mistaken for a food critic's review. I've stressed throughout this whole book that the personal statement should be about you—it's not a research paper, the synopsis of an event, or an exposé of your childhood friend. Jeremy is breaking this cardinal rule and writing a personal statement about olives. This is a tangent risk, since in going off on a tangent, he could potentially waste his whole word count on a subject that tells admissions officers absolutely nothing about him.

Why I Still Encouraged the Risk

I knew Jeremy's B– average didn't tell the full story; he might have struggled in the classroom, but he also had a beaming personality and genuine intellectual curiosity he needed to put on display. I also believed the olive extended metaphor could be fun and make a lasting impression on admissions officers who might think his numbers weren't high enough. As an Average Joe, Jeremy would have to work a little harder to be considered, and that is what made this risk worth taking.

There seems to be no middle ground when it comes to olives. People either love them or hate them. Those who hate them *really* hate them, complaining that they are too mushy or too salty. Some even say that eating an olive feels like ingesting pure seawater. I suppose I understand this. After all, olives do have a distinctly oily texture and an intense, sour smell. Then there is the pit factor, which poses a threat to the teeth. For better or for worse, though, I am a champion of olives. My favorite variety is the Kalamata olive, which is native to Greece. The bitter taste is surprisingly satisfying, and the pit allows me to savor just one at a time. Yet for me, an olive is not just a snack; it represents much more.

While growing up, I had the opportunity to sample many Mediterranean foods, the most important of which was olives. My Greek heritage may have exposed me to olives at an early age, but I've become a connoisseur on my own. I can't remember a moment when I opened the refrigerator and did not see olives in there. I was initially afraid of them, believing that they looked a little too much like eyeballs, but I warmed up to them over time. During baseball season, my dad would often come home from work and sit down to watch a Rangers game with a bowl of olives balanced on his knee. Olives were even a huge staple at my grandmother's house, where everything, from salads to baked bread, was accented with the fruit.

I'm positive and open to trying new things regardless of the outcome, and this trait has prompted culinary experimentation. While some undertakings, like my olive milkshake attempt, were ill fated, other endeavors have yielded more promising results. My optimism has also impacted how I approach academics. This past summer, I decided to participate in a weeklong neuroscience program at [name of college] to study the effects of certain substances, such as caffeine, on the brain. I really didn't know what to expect from the program because I had never explored the subject, but I went for it and ended up excelling both in class discussions and on my final project. Not everything comes as easily to me, though. My dyslexia has put up a few roadblocks, but I see it as a great opportunity to test my creativity. Much like trying to bake olives into brownies, approaching my studies in a visual way is difficult, but doable, and ultimately very rewarding. I had my doubts, too, but those brownies were surprisingly delicious. I take the initiative to find ways to relate to the material in all my classes, a task that requires imagination and a little trial and error. I think in images rather than numbers and words, and drawing pictures of certain information is surprisingly effective when it comes to comprehending poems and deciphering trigonometry problems. Similarly, rather than fighting the onslaught of olives in my mother's cooking, I embraced them as an ingredient that accents and enhances the many foods I love.

My approach to learning is similar, as I embrace my different style through experimentation. There is usually a unique path to solving every problem and to creating every new recipe, and it's exciting to figure it out. I sometimes wonder how my bread, omelets, and spaghetti sauce would taste without olives. I can only imagine it would be a bleak landscape for my taste buds. Likewise, traits that have been labeled learning "disabilities" actually make my personality resolute and positive.

Why this approach worked:

+ Through his use of olives as a narrative device, Jeremy is able to depict his dyslexia as an asset that gives him a creative perspective and pushes him to be resourceful, rather than a setback he needs to self-consciously explain. From the very first line, the essay is playful and wholly unexpected, and that's what keeps readers engaged.

+ It's also interesting that through this risk, Jeremy fulfilled his Average Joe imperative and angle. He acknowledges that he is really starting to get his academic footing, and although he has to try a bit harder in his classes, his interest is sincere. The essay is teeming with optimism and anticipation, which will leave the impression that he's ready to hit the ground running in college.

Jeremy was unexpectedly accepted to a few of the reach schools on his college list.

STUDENT 6: AARON (ACHIEVE-O-TRON)

Aaron liked FPS (First Person Shooter) video games, such as *Call of Duty*, and spent much of his time in his boarding school dorm room, eyes glued to his screen. Looking at his transcript, I worried that too many of his activities—computer programming, cyber security competitions, Biology Olympiad, the Siemens Competition—were solitary. It's important that students defy stereotypes in their essays, recognizing their student type so they can show how they are so much more. Thus I had to veto all of Aaron's dry, academically based suggestions that made him seem like a know-it-all. I could tell that he was a congenial guy, so I asked about the role he played in his social group: Was he good at doing impressions? Was he a trivia guru? It turns out he had a very distinctive laugh, the kind you could pick out of a crowd, and his friends were endlessly amused by it. When it came time to crank out his essays, he decided to write about his ability to laugh at himself, hoping to infuse his impressive but predictable application with "oomph."

Why This Approach Was Risky

The humility mandated by Aaron's Achieve-o-Tron status needed to be genuine, yet this approach set him up to do the "humble brag." If the self-effacing humor had merely underscored how good he was at everything or had served as self-promotion, it would have sounded obnoxious. Additionally, writing about laughter could have easily ended up like a *Seinfeld* episode: amusing, but ultimately about nothing at all. He had to apply laughter to substantive experiences.

Why I Still Encouraged the Risk

Aaron's application desperately needed some personality, as well as a social element. I figured that with laughter, he could demonstrate how he interacts with others and could avoid describing himself alone at his computer at odd hours of the night.

My friends love to tease that when I'm watching *The Big Bang Theory* on Thursday nights, the first floor of our dorm resonates with my rapid-fire, staccato laughter. While I cannot produce the full, round syllables of Santa's boisterous hoot, I can actually laugh and talk at the same time, undulating my sentences even as I discuss rotational motion problem sets. When I first arrived at boarding school, I wasn't even aware that I had this habit until my roommate Alex told me how my lightheartedness had immediately put him at ease on move-in day. Climbing to the fourth floor with boxes and luggage put most of our hall mates in a frustrated, frenzied state, yet when I dropped my suitcase and the zipper popped, spewing my belongings down an entire flight of stairs, I unexpectedly responded with laughter and relaxed the tension.

In laughing at myself, I have always been able to move forward instead of agonizing over disappointments. For instance, in third grade, I spent a week assembling a rubber-band-propelled model airplane to compete in the school-wide science competition. When it was my turn to toss my model off the top of the soccer field bleachers, I accidentally broke off the tail while winding the propeller. Since there was no time to make adjustments, I simply had to laugh off my misfortune when the plane plummeted straight down and tragically broke in half on impact. "Oh well. I guess the tail is important, after all," I joked as I went to retrieve the wreckage. The teachers breathed an audible sigh of relief and surprise, as many tears had been shed that day over aviation failures.

My habit of finding unexpected humor also came in handy in my freshman year, when my gangly, pre-growth-spurt frame made me ideal, according to three seniors, for wrestling in the 103 lb. category. Needing teammates for the lightest weight class, they begged me until I agreed to try out despite my reservations. I must have jinxed myself during my first two minutes on the mat against my 120 lb. teammate, because the moment I realized I was actually having fun, my attempt at a takedown went awry and I felt a searing, wrenching pain in my left wrist. When my teammate rolled off of my hand, silence fell over the gym and the whole team waited for me to scream or maybe even cry. Instead, finding the fact that I had fractured my wrist to be oddly comical, I started laughing. "Who would have thought that being 103 pounds wouldn't make me a he-man!" was my punch line as the trainer announced that I'd need to wear a plaster cast for three weeks.

I've been told by my teachers that my BB gun laugh keeps dialogue lively and fluid in the classroom, and when I tutor, my laughter also helps lighten the mood so my students feel more comfortable asking questions. It is Leonard, though, the physicist on my favorite Thursday night show, who elicits my loudest, most rippled chuckle, as he tries to explain social niceties to his scientist roommates. I feel as if I play an opposite, but relatable role, in my own life, clarifying programming jokes for my dorm mates.

Why this approach worked:

+ Yes, there is a bit of humble bragging scattered throughout the essay, but Aaron manages to keep his voice likeable.
+ He shows how he relates to, and amuses, others—which nicely complements a transcript full of solitary intellectual endeavors.

Several Ivy League admissions committees certainly appreciated his buoyancy.

STUDENT 7: JAMESON (NATURAL)

Jameson had the transcript of an Achieve-o-Tron, but his trademark all-too-casual look and laid-back demeanor made him more of a Natural. He was immensely likeable, but he still worried, as many Naturals do, that he would seem as if he didn't care. He didn't want to sound uptight, either, because being buttoned-up just wasn't his style. Jameson was highly involved in debate, and when he wasn't arguing his own cases, he volunteered to teach kids effective public speaking and research skills; despite his devotion, his original draft on debate was boring and stuffy. So, scrapping his straightforward outline, he decided to embrace his sartorial sloppiness and write an essay on how people refer to him as a "bum."

Why This Approach Was Risky

Do I even have to explain? Calling yourself a "bum" is a "throwing yourself under the bus" type of risk, because defying social norms is quirky and interesting only half the time. Moreover, this is a particularly bad classification that can signify laziness, insensitivity, disrespect, or all of the above.

Why I Still Encouraged the Risk

Jameson wanted to defend his style as a deliberate and thoughtful decision, not simply say, "This is who I am. Take it or leave it." I knew that as long as he wasn't combative or defensive, the essay stood a chance. To set the right tone, he had to poke fun at himself, and luckily he was willing to do that.

> Ever since the seventh grade, my friends, teachers, and even my own parents have all teasingly labeled me a "bum." This moniker was not a commentary on my personal hygiene, but on the fact that at any given moment and under any weather forecast, I would don casual sweatpants, slippers, and baggy T-shirts.
>
> Choosing to wear sandals with my white Adidas socks was initially met with confused stares and stifled laughter from my better-attired friends. Unaffected, I simply smiled back and reminded them that I was not breaking any dress code and that what I wear does not affect my performance in the classroom. In fact, this personal style arose after my mom finally surrendered complete control of my wardrobe to me, because I would rather spend my time pondering the tenets of existentialism as laid out by author John Gardner, than wondering whether an Abercrombie & Fitch T-shirt would complement a pair of True Religion Brand Jeans.
>
> However, spending too much time in my own enclosed comfort zone, I have learned the hard way that wearing sweatpants is not

appropriate for every situation. For example, at my first debate tournament, I embarrassed my team by showing up in baggy, gray Nike trainer pants and an oversized American Eagle hoodie. My coach threatened to remove me from the team, but I argued that the league constitution did not actually mandate business formal. After pleading that what I wore would not detract from the quality of my arguments nor elicit penalties from the judges, I convinced my coach to let me to compete with only five minutes remaining before my match. While my opponents deridingly snickered amongst themselves because I was not wearing a tie, after the first few minutes, they began focusing on what I was saying instead of what I was wearing. To my coach's surprise, I won both rounds of the debate. Nevertheless, for future debates, I extracted the suit from the back of my closet.

Then again, there have been several times when dressing down has worked to my advantage. One instance is when I taught debate to students at a local middle school. Because my casual dress code helped break the traditional teacher-student paradigm, all twelve of the students—ranging from introverted Daniel to restless, athletic Michael—felt comfortable speaking up. Moreover, because I built a relaxed atmosphere, they easily embraced the intellectual role that debaters must assume when tackling pressing issues, such as whether the United States federal government should or should not substantially increase its space exploration.

While virtually all teenagers face the incessant criticism from their parents of, "Are you really leaving the house looking like that?" people who know me have truly embraced the idea that the value of a man is not based on what designer brand he wears. When and if I one day have avid readers of *Vogue* and *The Sartorialist* breathing down my neck, I will remind them to take a look at two of my generation's icons: Mark Zuckerberg, with his signature hoodie and Adidas sandals, and Steve Jobs, who was rumored to have had over 100 identical, black turtlenecks hanging in his closet.

Although my first inclination will be to wear my favorite Knicks jersey to the school prom, I know that eventually I'll have to yield to social etiquette and routinely wear my Sunday best on a more regular basis. Fortunately, I'll have some time, as I doubt my Spanish and history professors will expect that from me just yet.

Why this approach worked:

+ Jameson stays true to himself and simultaneously uses this seemingly negative trait to his advantage.
+ There are times when readers might worry he is veering into judgmental territory, but he acknowledges cultural norms and the necessity of appropriate compromise as he enters professional settings.
+ He draws attention to his debate skills without resorting to bragging.

Jameson was accepted to twelve of the thirteen institutions to which he applied, many of which were Ivy League schools.

The level of "risk" is different for each person, so I don't want you to use these examples as templates; instead, get inspired by their creativity to find something that fits your own style and student type.

CHAPTER 11

WRAP IT UP

+ A FEW FINAL POINTERS +

1. No general philosophizing—you're seventeen. Get over yourself. Sorry for the tough love, but you really have to base your observations on experiences you've had. Nobody likes a teenage know-it-all.

2. Don't just narrate events and facts—integrate emotion, reactions, and personalization so admissions officers can get a better sense of your personality. Note the differences:

"I won the award."

Versus:

"I was both surprised and overjoyed to learn that I had won first place."

Or . . .

"Smith is part of the five-school consortium, so I would have access to an even greater number of resources."

Versus:

"I was thrilled to discover that Smith is part of the five-school consortium, meaning that I can add classics courses at Bryn Mawr or economics classes at Amherst to my schedule."

Or . . .

"Johns Hopkins has a global perspective."

Versus:

"I admire how Johns Hopkins emphasizes sustainability and global-mindedness in its engineering program, since these are two factors I value. I am also drawn to the unique interdisciplinary approach that supplements engineering studies with humanities and social sciences. The fact that the core requirements include Introduction to Business within the Civil Professional Practice courses shows me that Johns Hopkins wants its engineers to be able to not only hone their technical skills, but also develop marketing and manufacturing know-how to ensure that their ideas are viable. Overall, the civil engineering department would be the perfect home for my inquisitive mind, my focus on limiting environmental impact, and my drive to combine aesthetic appeal with functionality."

You get the point.

3. Always have several sets of eyes look over your essay. People who haven't been reading and rereading your drafts are more likely than you are to catch errors. In addition to getting an editor—probably a teacher or guidance counselor—to look it over, ask a classmate you don't know very well to read it. Afterward, ask what they were able to learn about you.

I hope that you found this guide helpful! Best of luck, and remember:

+ Humility
+ Honesty
+ Humor

I would like to thank the following people:

My agent, Laurie Abkemeier, who believed in this book from the moment I pitched it to her and offered invaluable advice along the way.

My editor, Lisa Westmoreland, who helped this book come to life and made it better with each step.

The wonderful and brilliant students whom I've been lucky to mentor over the years, especially those whose profiles, writing, and successes are featured in this guide.

My Olympiad family—Mrs. Lee, Stella, Rod, Thomas, James—who showed me the ropes.

My amazing parents, who have always supported my writing aspirations—I promise the magical realism novel is still in the works.

My in-laws, who generously babysat so I could write and edit.

My husband, Matt, who makes all things interesting and hilarious and possible.

My beautiful daughter, Parker, who will hopefully use this guide somewhere down the road.

©Roger Kriegel

ASHLEY WELLINGTON is the founder of Mint Tutors LLC (MintTutors.com), an online educational community that specializes in academic tutoring, college guidance, and test preparation. It is based out of New York City, but caters to students across the globe.

Wellington grew up in Dallas, Texas. As an undergraduate at Princeton, she was the recipient of the Theodore Weiss Creative Writing Award. She was then awarded a scholarship from the Ernest L. Ransome Trust to attend graduate school at the University of St. Andrews in Scotland. There she earned a master's degree with distinction in creative writing. Wellington then tutored for several elite agencies, including Metro Academic Prep (MAP), the Tutoring Collective, and Olympiad Academia, before founding Mint Tutors in 2010. Her interests include teaching, competitive running, hiking, and being with her family.

**DON'T STALK THE
ADMISSIONS OFFICER**

*How to Survive the College
Admissions Process Without
Losing Your Mind*
by Risa Lewak
208 pages, $13.99 paper (Can $16.99)
Paperback ISBN: 978-1-58008-060-6
eBook ISBN: 978-1-58008-382-9

OUTSMARTING THE SAT

*An Expert Tutor Reveals Her
Proven Techniques, Strategies,
and Confidence-Building Exercises
That Will Maximize Your Score*
by Elizabeth King
336 pages, $17.99 paper (Can $20.99)
Paperback ISBN: 978-1-58008-927-2
eBook ISBN: 978-1-58008-569-5

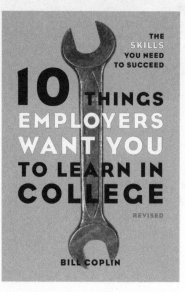

10 THINGS EMPLOYERS WANT YOU TO LEARN IN COLLEGE

REVISED
The Skills You Need to Succeed
by Bill Coplin
272 pages, $14.99 paper (Can $17.99)
Paperback ISBN: 978-1-60774-145-9
eBook ISBN: 978-0-307-76849-0

COLLEGE RULES!

THIRD EDITION
*How to Study, Survive, and
Succeed in College*
by Sherrie Nist-Olejnik, PhD,
and Jodi Patrick Holschuh, PhD
352 pages, $14.99 paper (Can $16.99)
Paperback ISBN: 978-1-60774-001-8
eBook ISBN: 978-1-60774-017-9